MEDITATION IN 10 MINUTES - THE PATH TO INNER PEACE IN 27 CHAPTERS

MR JEAN MICHEL PEREIRA DA SILVA

Copyright © 2023 Jean Michel P.s. All rights reserved. No part of this book may be reproduced or transmitted in any form or by any means, electronic or mechanical, including photocopying, recording, or any information storage and retrieval system, without the written permission of the author.

INDEX:

Introduction to meditation in 10 minutes
1. The history of meditation: from its origins to the West
2. The benefits of meditation: mind, body and spirit
3. The different techniques of meditation: a complete panorama
4. Preparation for meditation: environment, posture and breathing
5. Guided Meditation: The Power of Words
6. Mindfulness Meditation: The Art of Mindfulness
7. Vipassana Meditation: the meditation of insight
8. Zen Meditation: The Way of Silence

9. Transcendental Meditation: Beyond the Mind
10. Metta Meditation: Developing love and compassion
11. Breathing meditation: find inner balance
12. Walking Meditation: Awareness in motion
13. Visualization Meditation: Creating Positive Mental Images
14. Mandala Meditation: The Universe in a Circle
15. Meditation sounds and mantras: the power of vibrations
16. Yoga Nidra Meditation: Conscious Sleep
17. Meditation and creativity: the encounter between art and silence
18. Meditation and sports: improve physical and mental performance
19. Meditation and work: managing stress and increasing productivity
20. Meditation and relationships: cultivating empathy and

communication
21. Meditation and health: preventing and curing diseases
22. Meditation and aging: the secret of longevity
23. Mediation for children: develop awareness and social-emotional skills
24. Meditation for pregnant women: posture and breathing
25. Meditation and Spirituality: The Path to Enlightenment
26. Integrate meditation into daily life
27. Consolidate your meditation practice: useful advice and resources

INTRODUCTION

In a busy world full of distractions, finding inner peace has become a basic need for our mental, physical and spiritual health. Meditation is a millenary practice which, in recent times, has attracted growing interest thanks to its many scientifically proven benefits.

"Meditation in 10 Minutes: The Path to Inner Peace in 25 Chapters" is a book that will guide you step by step in learning and deepening meditation, with a particular focus on daily practice of just 10 minutes. This book is designed for anyone who wants to start or deepen meditation, regardless of their religious or philosophical beliefs.

The text is divided into 25 chapters, each of which deals with a specific aspect of meditation, from its historical origins to the different techniques, from the benefits to the relationship with creativity, sport, work, relationships and health. At the end of each chapter, you'll find practical exercises and tips to help you put what you've learned into practice and integrate meditation into your daily life.

In the first chapter, "Introduction to Meditation in 10 Minutes", we will introduce you to the fundamental principles of meditation and the basics to start practicing it in just 10 minutes a day. You will discover how meditation can help you find inner peace, manage stress and improve the quality of your life.

In the second chapter, "The history of meditation: from its origins to the West", we will explore the historical roots of meditation and its development over the centuries, up to its arrival in the West and its diffusion in the modern world.

In the third chapter, "The benefits of meditation: mind, body and spirit", we will delve into the many benefits that meditation offers on a mental, physical and spiritual level, with particular attention to the scientific evidence that supports its practice.

Starting from the fourth chapter, we will analyze the different meditation techniques, illustrating the characteristics of each one and providing practical examples to learn how to practice them. You will thus discover that there are multiple approaches to meditation, and you will be able to choose the one that best suits your needs and preferences.

In subsequent chapters, we will address specific topics related to meditation, such as the relationship between meditation and creativity, sports, work, relationships and health. In each of these chapters, you will find concrete examples of how meditation can be applied in different contexts to improve your well-being and that of the people around you.

Finally, in the twenty-seventh chapter, "Consolidating your meditation practice: useful tips and resources", we will provide you with suggestions for maintaining your meditation practice over time and for further deepening your knowledge of meditation, with the help of books, courses, apps and other resources available.

This book is designed as a path of personal growth, a journey to discover meditation and its benefits, with the aim of helping you find inner peace and improve the quality of your life. We hope it can become a valuable ally on your journey towards well-being and inner harmony. Happy reading and good practice!

CHAPTER 1: THE HISTORY OF MEDITATION: FROM ITS ORIGINS TO THE WEST

Meditation is a millenary practice that has its roots in different cultures and spiritual traditions from all over the world. To fully understand its scope and significance, it is important to explore the history of meditation and how it has developed over the centuries.

The origins of meditation date back thousands of years, with the earliest evidence of meditative practices being found in the ancient civilizations of India, China and Egypt. In the Indian subcontinent, meditation was already practiced within the Vedic tradition, around 1500 BC However, it is with Buddhism and Hinduism that meditation has taken a central role in spirituality and the quest for enlightenment.

Buddhism, founded by Prince Siddhartha Gautama (the Buddha) in the fifth century BC, considers meditation as one of the fundamental tools for achieving liberation from suffering and the attainment of Nirvana. In Buddhism, there are several meditation techniques, including mindfulness meditation (Vipassana) and metta (loving-kindness) meditation.

At the same time, Hinduism has also developed a rich corpus of meditative practices, linked in particular to Yoga and its eight "members" (Ashtanga Yoga) described by Patanjali in his Yoga Sutras. In Hinduism, meditation is seen as a means to bring about union between the individual and the divine, between the individual self (atman) and the universal self (Brahman).
Meanwhile, in China, Taoism and Confucianism have developed their own forms of meditation, centered around finding balance between yin and yang, harmony with nature, and the cultivation of moral virtues. Among the different Chinese meditation techniques, Qi Gong and Tai Chi are particularly known for their combination of physical movements, breathing and focusing the mind.

Even Western spiritual traditions, such as Judaism, Christianity and Islam, have developed meditative practices, even if these have not had the same centrality and diffusion as Eastern traditions.

For example, contemplative prayer in the Christian tradition, kabbalistic meditation in Judaism, and Sufism in Islam have profound meditative elements.

Since the 20th century, meditation has begun to spread in the West thanks to the growing interest in Eastern philosophies and practices, both in the spiritual and scientific fields.

Figures such as Swami Vivekananda, Paramahansa Yogananda and Maharishi Mahesh Yogi have played a fundamental role in the introduction of meditation and Yoga in the Western world, helping to create a dialogue between different cultures and traditions.

In the 1960s and 1970s, meditation was the subject of increasing curiosity and experimentation, especially in the context of

the counterculture and peace and social justice movements. Personalities such as Alan Watts, Ram Dass and Thich Nhat Hanh have helped spread the knowledge of meditation and promote its value as a tool for personal and social transformation.
Parallel to the spiritual interest, meditation has begun to attract the attention of the scientific community, with the first studies on its neurological and psychophysiological implications conducted by researchers such as Herbert Benson and Jon Kabat-Zinn. These studies have demonstrated the many benefits of meditation, including reducing stress, lowering blood pressure, improving focus, and increasing emotional resilience.

The growing scientific evidence base has helped to legitimize meditation in the eyes of the Western public and to promote its integration in various fields, such as medicine, psychology, education and the world of work. In particular, Mindfulness Meditation has become one of the most popular and studied techniques, thanks to its applicability to a wide range of contexts and problems.

Today, meditation is practiced by millions of people around the world, both as an integral part of their spirituality and as a tool to improve the quality of life and psychophysical well-being. Furthermore, meditation continues to be the object of study and experimentation, with new research that deepens its understanding and expands its applications.

In conclusion, the history of meditation shows us how this ancient practice has been able to evolve and adapt to different cultures and traditions over the centuries, while maintaining its fundamental core: the search for inner harmony and enlightenment. In an age of increasing stress and disconnection, meditation can act as a bridge between the past and the present, giving us the tools to face the challenges of modern life with wisdom and compassion.

CHAPTER 2: THE BENEFITS OF MEDITATION: MIND, BODY, AND SPIRIT

Meditation is a millenary practice that offers numerous benefits on a mental, physical and spiritual level. Thanks to scientific research, today we know better the positive effects of meditation on our daily life. In this chapter, we will look at the main benefits of meditation and propose an in-depth, practical exercise for you to try.

1. Reducing Stress and Anxiety: Practicing meditation helps calm the mind, reducing the negative thoughts and worries that often underlie stress and anxiety.

2. Improved concentration and memory: Meditation promotes focused attention, helping us to be more present in the moment and to develop better short- and long-term memory.

3. Increased empathy and compassion: Meditation helps us develop greater awareness of our own emotions and those of others, facilitating mutual understanding and

acceptance.

4. Improved physical well-being: Meditation has positive effects on physical health, helping to reduce blood pressure, improve sleep quality and strengthen the immune system.

5. Spiritual Development: Meditation can facilitate connection with the inner self and foster personal growth, helping us to better understand our purpose in life and develop a sense of oneness with others and with the universe.

Practice exercise: Integrated Awareness Meditation
The goal of this exercise is to combine the benefits of meditation for mind, body, and spirit into a single, in-depth practice.

1. Find a quiet, comfortable place to sit or lie down, with your back straight but relaxed.

2. Close your eyes and pay attention to your breath. Observe your breath without judgment, without trying to change it. Simply notice how the air moves in and out of your nostrils.

3. After a few minutes of observing your breath, start shifting your attention to the physical sensations present in every part of your body, starting from your feet and slowly going up to your head.

4. Once the body scan is complete, bring your attention to your heart and the emotions you are feeling at the moment. Welcome these emotions without judgment, letting them flow freely.

5. Now, imagine yourself radiating love and compassion towards yourself and others. Visualize this love as a light that spreads from you and reaches all the people around you, until it pervades the entire universe.

6. Conclude the exercise by returning to your breath and observing it for a few minutes, before slowly reopening your eyes and returning to your daily life.
7. Spend at least 15-20 minutes on this exercise, trying to practice it regularly to get more lasting and significant results.

Remember that meditation is a practice that requires time and dedication. The benefits come on gradually, but can have a profound and lasting impact on your life.

Maintaining consistency and patience are key to fully experiencing the benefits of meditation.

CHAPTER 3: THE DIFFERENT TECHNIQUES OF MEDITATION: A COMPLETE PANORAMA

Meditation is an ancient practice that has developed into different forms and traditions over the centuries. In this chapter, we'll explore some of the more popular meditation techniques and their benefits, offering a comprehensive overview of the different possibilities available to you.

At the end of the chapter, we will propose an in-depth exercise to experiment with one of the techniques described.

1. Mindfulness Meditation: This technique focuses on non-judgmental observation of the thoughts, emotions, and physical sensations that arise in the present moment. Mindfulness meditation can help reduce stress, improve focus, and increase empathy.

2. Transcendental Meditation: This technique involves using a mantra (a word or phrase repeated mentally) to focus the mind and transcend its activity. Transcendental Meditation has been associated with reduced stress, improved psychological well-being and increased creativity.

3. Loving-Kindness Meditation (Metta): This technique consists of generating feelings of love and compassion towards oneself, towards others and ultimately towards all sentient beings. Metta practice can help improve empathy, compassion, and interpersonal connection.

4. Vipassana Meditation: This meditation technique, also known as introspection meditation, focuses on deeply understanding reality through direct observation of one's mental and physical experiences. The practice of Vipassana can lead to greater self-awareness and liberation from mental suffering.

5. Zen Meditation (Zazen): This form of meditation originates in the Zen Buddhist tradition and focuses on posture, breathing, and observing thoughts without attachment. Zen meditation can help develop patience, concentration, and mindfulness.

In-depth exercise: Vipassana Meditation
In this exercise, we will guide you through a Vipassana meditation practice, ideal for deepening your awareness of yourself and your inner experiences.

1. Sit in a comfortable position, with your back straight and your hands on your legs or knees.

2. Close your eyes and begin focusing on your breathing, noticing how the air moves in and out of your nostrils.

3. Now, bring your attention to the physical sensations arising in your body, without judging them or trying to

change them. Pay attention to sensations of heat, cold, tension, relaxation, pain, or pleasure.

4. Then move on to observing your emotions, acknowledging and welcoming each emotion that arises, without judgment or resistance. Be aware of emotions such as joy, sadness, anger, fear or love.

5. Finally, observe your thoughts like clouds passing in the sky of the mind. Don't try to stop them or follow them, just acknowledge them and let them go.

6. Continue to practice this Vipassana meditation, alternating your attention between physical sensations, emotions and thoughts, always maintaining an attitude of non-judgment and acceptance.

7. Practice this meditation for at least 20 minutes. With time and regular practice, you will be able to develop a greater awareness of yourself and your inner experiences, improving your ability to handle life's challenges with greater balance and serenity.

This chapter has given you a complete overview of the different meditation techniques available, each with its own benefits and particularities. Experimenting with different techniques will allow you to find the one that best suits you and your needs, helping you to develop a solid and profound meditation practice.

CHAPTER 4: PREPARATION FOR MEDITATION: ENVIRONMENT, POSTURE AND BREATHING

Before diving into the different meditation techniques, it is important to take some time to understand how to properly prepare for meditation practice. In this chapter, we'll look at three key aspects of preparing for meditation: the environment, posture, and breathing. At the end of the chapter, we'll walk you through a hands-on exercise to familiarize yourself with these key elements.

1. Environment: A suitable environment for meditation can make a big difference in the quality of your practice. Here are some tips for creating an ideal space for meditation:

- Find a quiet, distraction-free place, preferably away from noise and interruptions.

- Keep the space neat and tidy to promote concentration and inner calm.
- If you wish, you can add elements such as candles, incense or sacred objects to create an atmosphere of serenity and spirituality.
- Make sure you have a comfortable chair, cushion (zafu), or mat to sit on during your meditation.

2. Posture: Posture plays a crucial role in meditation, as a correct position facilitates concentration and harmony between mind and body. Here are some guidelines for adopting good posture during meditation:

- Sit with your back straight and elongated, keeping your neck and head in line with your spine.
- If you meditate on a cushion (zafu), try to sit cross-legged in a stable and comfortable position. If you prefer, you can also use a chair with your feet planted on the floor and your knees bent at 90 degrees.
- Relax your shoulders, arms and hands, placing your hands on your legs or knees.
- Keep your chin slightly down and your face relaxed. You can keep your eyes closed or half closed, staring at an imaginary spot on the floor in front of you.

3. Breathing: Breathing is a key element in meditation, as it connects the mind and body and promotes concentration and inner calm. Here are some tips for proper meditative breathing:

- Breathe naturally, without forcing or controlling your breath.
- Bring your attention to the sensation of air flowing in and out of your nostrils or mouth.

- If it helps, you can count your breaths to stay focused and not get carried away by thoughts.

Practical exercise: Familiarize yourself with the environment, posture and breathing

1. Prepare your meditation environment by following the guidelines outlined above.
2. Sit in a comfortable position with a good posture, following the recommendations provided in the section on posture.
3. Begin to bring your attention to your breathing, watching the air go in and out of your nose or mouth.
4. Now, try to connect the three elements – environment, posture and breathing – in your meditation practice. Maintain awareness of your meditation space, correct posture, and natural, relaxed breathing.
5. Meditate for at least 10 minutes, focusing on your breathing and trying to maintain mindfulness.
6. At the end of the meditation, take a moment to reflect on the experience and notice any differences in your focus, inner calm, and mindfulness.

Remember that the key to effective meditation is consistent practice and dedication over time. Continue to work on your environment, posture and breathing to deepen your meditative experience and experience the many benefits this practice has to offer.

CHAPTER 5: GUIDED MEDITATION: THE POWER OF WORDS

Guided meditation is a form of meditation that uses words and narratives to help the practitioner achieve a state of relaxation and inner awareness.

This type of meditation can be practiced alone, following audio or video recordings, or in a group with an instructor who guides the session.

Guided meditation offers several advantages over other meditation techniques, including:

1. Ease of use: Guided meditation is often more accessible for beginners, providing a structured path and clear instructions on what to do as you practice.

2. Better concentration: Listening to the words of a guide can help you stay focused and keep your mind from wandering.

3. Personalization: Guided meditation can be tailored to the specific needs and interests of the practitioner, providing a more personalized and relevant experience.

4. Emotional Support: The words and narratives used in guided meditation can offer comfort and emotional support, particularly during times of stress or difficulty.

Guided meditation draws on the power of words to create immersive and transformative experiences. The words used during a guided meditation session are carefully chosen to evoke images, emotions and sensations that facilitate the meditation practice. Furthermore, words can have a profound impact on our mental and emotional state and help us achieve a state of relaxation and awareness.

In guided meditation, words are often used in conjunction with other techniques such as visualization, breathing focus, and body scanning.

This integrated approach allows you to create a richer and deeper meditation experience, facilitating access to altered states of consciousness and promoting general well-being.

Some key elements of the power of words in guided meditation include:

1. Intention: The words used during a guided meditation are chosen with particular attention to the intention and the meaning they convey. This can help create a supportive and welcoming atmosphere during your practice.

2. Rhythm and Tone: The pace and tone of words can affect our mental and emotional state. A calm and reassuring tone, combined with a slow and even rhythm, can promote relaxation and concentration.

3. Repetition: Repetition of key phrases or concepts can help reinforce the effects of guided meditation, allowing the practitioner to immerse themselves more deeply in the experience.

4. Metaphors and Symbolism: The use of metaphors

and symbolism in storytelling can help create vivid and engaging images, allowing the practitioner to connect with deeper aspects of one's mind.

Practical exercise: Guided meditation for relaxation and mindfulness

In this exercise, we will walk you through a simple guided meditation to promote relaxation and present moment awareness.

1. Find a quiet, comfortable place to sit or lie down. Make sure you have good posture and are relaxed, but alert.

2. Close your eyes and start bringing your attention to your breathing. Observe the air flowing in and out of your nose or mouth, without trying to control or change it.

3. Now, imagine yourself in a safe and peaceful place, such as a deserted beach, a flower garden, or a lush forest. Feel the sounds, smells and sensations of this place, allowing you to fully immerse yourself in the experience.

4. As you continue to breathe deeply, imagine that each inhalation brings with it positive and relaxing energy, while each exhalation releases tension and worries.

5. Now, start exploring your body with your mind, starting at your head and slowly working your way down to your neck, shoulders, arms, chest, abdomen, legs, and finally your feet. With each step, try to release tension and stiffness, allowing your body to relax more and more.

6. When you're done exploring the body, bring your attention back to your breathing and to your quiet place. Spend a few minutes enjoying this feeling of calm and relaxation.

7. Finally, slowly begin to bring your awareness to your body and your surroundings. Slowly wiggle your fingers

and toes, stretch your neck and shoulders, and when you feel ready, gently open your eyes.

8. Take a moment to reflect on the guided meditation experience and notice how you feel physically, mentally, and emotionally.

This guided meditation can be practiced anytime you want to relax or increase your awareness of the present moment. You can also explore other guided meditations that focus on specific themes, such as managing stress, self-compassion, or releasing fears and worries.

Remember that constant practice is the key to reaping the benefits of guided meditation. Over time, you may find that your ability to relax and stay present improves dramatically, leading to greater inner peace and overall well-being.

CHAPTER 6: MINDFULNESS MEDITATION: THE ART OF MINDFULNESS

Mindfulness meditation, also known as mindfulness, is a practice that focuses on mindful, non-judgmental attention to the present moment. The main goal is to develop a greater awareness of one's internal and external experiences, such as thoughts, emotions, physical sensations and environmental stimuli.

This type of meditation can lead to numerous benefits, including increased self-awareness, better stress management, and an increased ability to respond to situations with emotional intelligence and compassion.

Mindfulness meditation can be practiced in a variety of ways, including:

1. Seated Meditation: This type of practice focuses on awareness of your breath, body, and thoughts while sitting in a comfortable position and with correct posture.

2. Walking Meditation: During this practice, the practitioner focuses on awareness of physical sensations

and internal experiences while walking slowly and with intention.

3. Body scan meditation: In this exercise, attention is brought to different parts of the body, one at a time, to develop greater awareness of physical sensations and tensions.

It's important to remember that mindfulness meditation is not a goal to be achieved, but rather a skill to be cultivated and honed over time. At first, you may find it difficult to keep your attention on your breath or body sensations, but with consistent practice, it will become easier and more natural.

Some suggestions for deepening your mindfulness meditation practice include:

1. Extend the length of your sessions: If you're comfortable with 5-10 minute sessions, try gradually extending the length of your meditations. Increasing the time spent in meditation can help you immerse yourself more deeply in the practice and strengthen your awareness.

2. Experiment with different techniques: There is no "one size fits all" for mindfulness meditation. Explore different techniques, such as walking meditation or body scan meditation, to find out which ones work best for you and your needs.

3. Practice mindfulness in your daily life: Try to integrate mindfulness into your daily activities, such as eating, driving, or computer work. This can help you cultivate a sense of presence and awareness at all times of the day.

4. Join a Meditation Group or Class: Joining a meditation group or attending a class can offer valuable support, accountability, and insights to enhance your mindfulness meditation practice.

5. Be kind to yourself: Remember that mindfulness meditation is a skill that takes time and practice to develop. Be patient and kind to yourself during the process, recognizing that it's normal to have wandering thoughts and distracted moments.

By incorporating these tips into your mindfulness meditation practice, you will be able to deepen your connection with the present moment and experience the many benefits associated with mindfulness meditation, including increased self-understanding, better management of emotions, and greater resilience in the face of challenges. of life.

Mindfulness meditation is a practice that has ancient roots and dates back thousands of years. It has been developed in several spiritual and philosophical traditions, including Buddhism, Hinduism and Taoism. Over time, this practice has evolved and adapted to different cultures and contexts, to become an important tool for mental and physical well-being in the modern world.

One of the fundamental aspects of mindfulness meditation is attention to the present moment. This mindful attention helps develop the ability to observe thoughts, emotions, and sensations without judgment, enabling you to recognize and accept your inner and outer experiences as they arise.

This acceptance does not mean resigning or not acting in the face of difficulties, but rather acquiring a greater understanding of oneself and one's reactions, allowing one to face challenges with greater balance and discernment.

Mindfulness meditation is also closely related to the concept of mindfulness. Mindfulness refers to the ability to be fully present and focused on what is happening in the here and now, without being distracted by thoughts of the past or worries about the future.

The practice of mindfulness meditation helps cultivate this

mindfulness, improving the ability to focus and fully experience every moment of life.

In addition to present-moment attention and mindfulness, mindfulness meditation also encourages the development of other important qualities, such as compassion, empathy, and self-acceptance. Through regular practice, one can learn to treat themselves and others with greater kindness and understanding, fostering healthier and more fulfilling relationships.

Finally, it is important to emphasize that mindfulness meditation is not an isolated practice, but can be integrated into other types of meditation or wellness practices.

For example, mindfulness meditation can be combined with concentration meditation, in which attention is focused on a specific object, such as a mantra or candle. Additionally, mindfulness meditation can be practiced alongside relaxation techniques, such as deep breathing or progressive muscle relaxation meditation.

Bottom line, mindfulness meditation is an art that requires dedication, patience, and constant practice. However, the resulting benefits can be profound and long-lasting, helping to improve quality of life, mental health and the general well-being.

Through the practice of mindfulness meditation, one can develop a greater connection with oneself, with others and with the world around us, promoting a sense of peace, balance and inner harmony.

To further deepen your mindfulness meditation practice, it helps to experiment with different meditation techniques and modalities. Some of the more common include:

1. Vipassana Meditation: This form of mindfulness meditation originates in the Theravada Buddhist tradition and is characterized by close observation of physical and mental sensations. Vipassana practice focuses on

exploring the interdependence of mind and body, leading to a greater understanding of the causes of pain and suffering.

2. Zen Meditation: Also known as Zazen, Zen meditation is a form of mindfulness meditation practiced in the Mahayana Buddhist tradition. This practice focuses on observing the mind without judgment, allowing one to develop greater clarity and awareness of one's internal experiences.

3. Loving-Kindness Meditation (Metta): This mindfulness meditation practice, also of Buddhist origin, focuses on sending love and kindness to yourself and others. Through the repetition of benevolent phrases, the sense of compassion and empathy is strengthened.

4. Walking meditation: Walking meditation is an alternative to sitting meditation and consists of walking slowly and with awareness, paying attention to each step and the sensations felt in the body during the movement.

Practical exercise: Breath awareness meditation

In this exercise, we will guide you through a simple mindfulness meditation based on attention to the breath.

1. Find a quiet, comfortable place to sit or lie down. Make sure your posture is correct and relaxed, but alert.

2. Close your eyes and pay attention to your breath. Don't try to control or change your breathing, but just observe it as it is.

3. Notice the sensations associated with inhaling and exhaling, such as cool air entering your nose and warm air leaving your mouth.

4. As your mind begins to wander, notice the thoughts that arise, and then gently bring your attention back to your breath.

5. Keep practicing for 5-10 minutes, or as long as feels comfortable.

6. When you're done, slowly open your eyes and take a moment to reflect on the mindfulness meditation experience and how it feels.

This breath awareness meditation can be practiced regularly to develop greater focus on the present moment and better management of emotions and stress. With consistent practice, you may find that your ability to stay aware and present increases dramatically, leading to greater inner peace and overall well-being.

CHAPTER 7: VIPASSANA MEDITATION: THE MEDITATION OF INSIGHT

Vipassana meditation, also known as insight meditation, is one of the oldest and most authentic meditation techniques, which has its roots in the Theravada Buddhist tradition.

The term "Vipassana" comes from Pali, an ancient language of India, and can be translated as "seeing things as they are" or "insight". The practice of Vipassana meditation aims to develop awareness and deep understanding of reality, helping to free oneself from suffering and achieve inner enlightenment.

Vipassana meditation is based on the careful and non-judgmental observation of the physical sensations, thoughts and emotions that emerge during the practice.

Instead of focusing on a single object of meditation, as occurs in other techniques, Vipassana encourages an open and inclusive awareness of all that presents itself to attention. This approach allows one to develop a deeper and more direct understanding of the impermanent, unsatisfying, and non-self nature of human experiences.

The practice of Vipassana meditation can be divided into three main stages:

1. Concentration: To begin the practice, it is important to develop some mental stability and concentration. This can be done by focusing attention on the breath, body sensations, or another object of meditation. Once a certain calm and focus has been achieved, one can proceed to the next stage.
2. Awareness: In this stage, attention is broadened to include all sensory, mental, and emotional experiences that arise during the practice. One closely observes physical sensations, thoughts and emotions without identifying with or judging them. The goal is to develop a clear and penetrating awareness of what is happening in the present moment.
3. Insight: With time and consistent practice, Vipassana meditation can lead to profound and transformative insights into the nature of reality and the self. These insights, or "insight," can help dissolve the illusions and attachments that cause suffering and develop greater inner freedom and lasting peace.

Vipassana meditation can be practiced both as a formal practice, through meditation retreats and courses, and as an informal practice, integrated into daily life. In both cases, it is important to approach the practice with an attitude of curiosity, openness and kindness towards oneself and one's experiences.

The practice of Vipassana meditation is a path of self-knowledge and inner transformation that develops through careful and non-judgmental observation of one's experiences. This meditative approach, which has its roots in the Theravada Buddhist tradition, has been handed down for millennia and has been shown to have numerous benefits for mental, emotional and spiritual health.

To deepen the practice of Vipassana meditation, it is useful to explore some key aspects that characterize this form of meditation:

1. The nature of attention: Vipassana meditation requires a particular quality of attention, which can be described as "clear and penetrating awareness". This type of awareness is different from focused concentration on a single object, as occurs in other forms of meditation. In Vipassana, attention is open, inclusive and non-selective, allowing one to observe and understand all experiences that arise in the field of awareness.

2. Observing the Three Universal Characteristics: A fundamental part of the practice of Vipassana meditation is the observation of the three universal characteristics of existence: impermanence (anicca), dissatisfaction (dukkha), and not-self (anatta). These characteristics are present in all human experiences and are considered the keys to understanding the true nature of reality. By observing these three characteristics through meditation practice, it is possible to develop a profound insight into reality and to dissolve the attachments that cause suffering.

3. The Importance of Continuous Practice: Vipassana meditation is a transformational journey that requires commitment and perseverance. Regular practice is essential to deepen your understanding of reality and develop greater inner freedom. Many practitioners of Vipassana meditation choose to participate in intensive meditation retreats, which offer the opportunity to fully immerse themselves in the practice and deepen one's experience. However, even daily practice at home can lead to significant changes and insights over time.

4. The importance of ethics and morality: Vipassana meditation is not only a mental practice, but also involves the ethical and moral aspect of life. According to Buddhist tradition, to develop a deep and authentic meditation practice, it is necessary to follow a life path based on morality, generosity and wisdom. This includes the observance of the five moral precepts (refrain from taking life, stealing, sexual misconduct, false speech, and use of intoxicants), which are considered essential for creating conditions conducive to the development of meditation and spiritual growth.

5. The relationship between Vipassana and other forms of meditation: Vipassana meditation is often practiced alongside other forms of meditation, such as mindfulness meditation and metta (loving-kindness) meditation. Mindfulness meditation, in particular, is closely related to Vipassana and can be considered an important foundation for developing the practice. Metta meditation, on the other hand, helps cultivate an attitude of love and compassion towards oneself and others, facilitating the integration of meditation practice into daily life.

6. Applying Vipassana in Daily Life: One of the goals of Vipassana meditation is to bring the awareness and understanding developed during the practice into everyday life. This means applying the principles of Vipassana meditation, such as non-judgmental observation and attention to the present moment, in all situations and challenges one encounters in life. This integration of meditation practice into daily life can lead to greater harmony and well-being, both personally and interpersonally.

To further delve into the practice of Vipassana meditation, it is advisable to seek guidance from an experienced teacher or join a meditation class. This can provide valuable instruction and support in your path of self-exploration and inner transformation. With commitment and dedication, Vipassana meditation can offer profound insights and benefits for the mind, body and spirit.

Practice Exercise for Chapter 7: Introduction to Vipassana Meditation

1. Find a quiet, distraction-free place where you can practice meditation. Sit on a chair, cushion, or mat with your back straight and your chin slightly tucked in.
2. Close your eyes and bring your attention to your breath. Notice the air flowing in and out of your nostrils and notice the sensations associated with the inhalation and exhalation. Continue to focus on your breath for a few minutes until you feel calm and focused.
3. Once you feel calm and focused, broaden your awareness to include all physical, mental, and emotional sensations that arise during your practice. Observe these experiences without judgment, trying to maintain an attitude of curiosity and openness to all that arises.
4. When you find your mind wandering or lost in thoughts and emotions, simply acknowledge what is happening and gently return your attention to your direct experience of the present moment.
5. Continue practicing Vipassana meditation for at least 10-15 minutes, or longer if desired. With time and consistent practice, you may begin to develop deeper insights into the nature of reality and the self, leading to greater inner freedom and well-being.

The practice of Vipassana meditation requires commitment, patience and dedication. It's normal to encounter challenges and resistance along the way, but it's important to remember that these obstacles are an integral part of the growth and learning process. Approach your practice with kindness and compassion, and you will find that Vipassana meditation can offer profound insights and transformations on your journey to inner peace and freedom from suffering.

CHAPTER 8: ZEN MEDITATION: THE WAY OF SILENCE

Zen meditation is a form of meditative practice that originates in the Mahayana Buddhist tradition, specifically the Japanese school of Zen Buddhism. The term "Zen" comes from the Sanskrit "dhyana", meaning "deep meditation", and reflects Zen practice's emphasis on meditation as a means of realizing the true nature of reality and freeing oneself from suffering.

Zen meditation is characterized by an attitude of simplicity, spontaneity and inner silence, which helps empty the mind of everyday thoughts and worries. In this chapter, we'll explore the key principles of Zen meditation and provide a hands-on exercise to get you started.

1. Posture and breathing: In Zen meditation, posture and breathing are fundamental elements. The traditional posture for Zen meditation is zazen, a cross-legged sitting position with a straight back. It is important to maintain a stable and relaxed posture, which allows you to stay balanced and concentrated during the practice. Instead, breathing should be natural and deep, with the diaphragm expanding on inhalation and contracting on exhalation.

2. Concentration and Mindfulness: In Zen meditation, the goal is to develop a calm and focused mind, free from thoughts and distractions. This is accomplished through concentration on an object of meditation, such as the breath, a mantra, or a koan (a riddle or paradoxical question used as a meditation tool). Constant attention and mindfulness allow you to immerse yourself in the depths of inner silence and experience the true nature of reality.

Zen meditation is a spiritual practice that aims to develop mindfulness, inner tranquility, and enlightenment through concentration and mindfulness. To deepen your understanding of Zen meditation, we'll look at some key aspects of Zen practice and philosophy.

1. History and origins of Zen: Zen Buddhism is a school of Mahayana Buddhism that developed in China in the 6th century AD, known as "Chan". Subsequently, it spread to Japan in the XII century, where it acquired the name "Zen". Zen practice is heavily influenced by Taoism and Buddhism from India, with an emphasis on meditation and direct realization of the nature of reality.
2. Fundamental Principles of Zen: The heart of Zen practice is meditation, or "zazen," which means "to sit in meditation." Zen meditation focuses on developing a calm, clear and present mind, which allows you to see reality as it is, without distortion or prejudice. Another fundamental principle of Zen is the importance of "non-attachment", or the ability to let go of beliefs, expectations and habits of mind that prevent you from seeing the truth.
3. Koans and Zen Practice: Koans are puzzles or paradoxical questions used in Zen practice to prompt the meditator to transcend logical and rational thinking and access a deeper and more intuitive understanding of reality. Famous koan

examples include "What is the sound of one hand?", "If you meet the Buddha on the road, kill him" and "What is your original face before your parents were born?".

4. Zen masters and monasteries: Zen practice is traditionally taught and transmitted by spiritual masters, called "roshis", who guide students on their path of development and enlightenment. Zen monasteries, or "zendo," are places of practice and learning, where students can immerse themselves in meditation practice, study Buddhist texts, and receive direct instruction from Zen masters.

5. Zen in Daily Life: In addition to the formal practice of meditation, Zen emphasizes the integration of awareness and mindfulness into daily life. This means practicing "non-attachment" and "beginner's mind" at all times, living with simplicity, humility and compassion. Some Zen practitioners also engage in forms of art and calligraphy as an expression of their spiritual practice.

Zen meditation is a profound and transformative practice that can lead to greater awareness, serenity, and an understanding of life. By deepening your Zen practice, you will be able to experience the benefits of meditation and develop a deeper connection with yourself and the world around you. As you progress on your Zen path, you may discover new dimensions of Zen practice and philosophy that will further enrich your spiritual experience.

6. The practice of walking meditation: Zen meditation is not limited to sitting practice. Walking meditation, or "kinhin," is another important aspect of Zen practice. During walking meditation, one tries to maintain the same awareness and mindfulness that is practiced during sitting meditation, focusing on the movement of the body and the sensation of the feet touching the ground. Walking meditation can be an effective tool for integrating meditation practice into daily life and for developing greater body awareness.

7. Work and Daily Life in Zen: Another central aspect of Zen practice is the integration of meditation and mindfulness into daily life, including work. In the monastic context, this is manifested through the practice of "samu", or manual work, which is done with the same mindfulness and attention that one devotes to meditation. Even in lay life, Zen practice encourages one to carry out one's work and daily activities with awareness, presence and compassion.

8. The Tea Ceremony in Zen: The Japanese tea ceremony, or "chado", is closely related to Zen practice and is an art that requires concentration, mindfulness, and a deep respect for others. The tea ceremony can be seen as an opportunity to practice meditation in motion and to cultivate harmony and connection with the other participants.

In conclusion, Zen meditation is a rich and profound practice that offers multiple benefits for the mind, body and spirit. As you deepen your practice and understand its core principles, you will experience greater awareness, tranquility, and connection with yourself and the world. Remember that Zen practice is not limited to sitting meditation, but can be integrated into all aspects of daily life, bringing greater presence and awareness to each moment.

Practical exercise: Zen meditation with the breath
To start your Zen meditation practice, follow these simple steps:

1. Find a quiet, comfortable place to practice meditation. Make sure you are free from distractions and that the environment is conducive to concentration and relaxation.

2. Sit in the zazen position, with your legs crossed and your back straight. If you prefer, you can also sit on a chair or meditation cushion, while still maintaining a stable and relaxed posture.

3. Close your eyes or fix them slightly down, keeping your

gaze soft and relaxed.

4. Bring your attention to your breath. Notice the flow of air going in and out of the nostrils and observe the movement of the diaphragm during inhalation and exhalation.

5. Whenever the mind wanders or gets lost in thought, just acknowledge the distraction and gently return your focus to your breath. Don't judge or criticize yourself for distractions; it is natural for the mind to wander, and the important thing is to recognize this fact and bring attention back to the breath.

6. Continue practicing Zen meditation for at least 10 minutes, or as long as you like. Try to maintain mindfulness and concentration throughout the practice, immersing yourself in the depths of inner silence.

7. Conclude the meditation by gradually bringing your attention to your body and surroundings. Take a moment to thank yourself for taking the time to practice meditation and the benefits it brings.

Regular practice of Zen meditation can lead to increased awareness, tranquility, and insight, as well as better stress management and a deeper sense of connection with yourself and others. As your practice deepens, you may also wish to explore other forms of Zen meditation, such as meditating on a mantra or koan, to further enrich your experience and spiritual development.

CHAPTER 9: TRANSCENDENTAL MEDITATION: BEYOND THE MIND

Transcendental Meditation is a meditation technique that originates in the Vedic tradition of ancient India and was brought to the attention of Western audiences in the 1950s and 60s by the Maharishi Mahesh Yogi. This form of meditation is notable for its simplicity and for its effectiveness in producing tangible benefits on the mental and physical health of the practitioners.

Transcendental meditation is based on the use of a mantra, or a word or phrase without a specific meaning, which is repeated mentally during meditation. The mantra is intended to help the meditator focus attention and facilitate the process of transcendence, i.e. the achievement of a deeper state of consciousness, detached from everyday thoughts and concerns.

One of the key aspects of Transcendental Meditation is the absence of effort and control. Unlike other meditation techniques, which often require intense concentration or the visualization of specific images, Transcendental Meditation encourages the practitioner to let the mantra flow freely in the mind, without attempting to control or manipulate it. In this way, the mind can gradually "immerse" in a state of deep relaxation and inner peace.

TM can be learned through structured courses, in which a qualified TM teacher assigns a personal mantra to the practitioner and guides him or her through the different stages of the practice. Generally, it is recommended that you practice Transcendental Meditation twice a day, for about 20 minutes per session.
Numerous scientific researches have highlighted the benefits of transcendental meditation for mental and physical health.

These include:

- Stress and Anxiety Reduction: Transcendental Meditation has been shown to reduce levels of the stress hormone cortisol and promote the release of neurotransmitters associated with well-being, such as serotonin and dopamine.
- Improved Cognitive Functions: Regular practice of Transcendental Meditation can help improve memory, attention and problem-solving skills.
- Lowering Blood Pressure: Some studies have shown that Transcendental Meditation can help lower blood pressure, reducing the risk of cardiovascular disease.
- Improved Sleep: Transcendental Meditation can help regulate circadian rhythms and relieve symptoms of insomnia.
- Increased Emotional Resilience: Transcendental Meditation can help strengthen your ability to cope with stress and emotional challenges, promoting a greater sense of inner balance.

In conclusion, transcendental meditation is a simple and effective practice that can bring many mental, emotional and physical benefits. To fully experience the benefits of this technique, it is important to take a course led by a qualified teacher and practice regularly.

However, even if you don't have access to a TM course, you can experience some of the benefits of this practice through mantra-based meditation, as described earlier. The key point to keep in mind is the importance of letting the mantra flow freely in the mind, without effort or control, thus allowing the mind to immerse itself in a state of deep relaxation and inner peace.

Transcendental Meditation is suitable for people of all ages and walks of life, and can be easily integrated into your daily routine. With consistent practice, you may notice significant improvements in your overall well-being and ability to handle the stresses and challenges of daily life.

Practical exercise. While it's recommended that you learn TM from a qualified teacher, you can try a simple mantra-based meditation exercise to get a feel for how the practice works.

1. Choose a quiet place without distractions, and sit comfortably with your back straight and your eyes closed.

2. Choose a mantra that is simple and meaningful to you, such as "Om" or "Peace." The mantra can be a word or phrase that helps focus your attention and facilitate relaxation.

3. Begin repeating the mantra silently in your mind, effortlessly and without trying to control the pace or cadence of the repetition. Let the mantra flow naturally in your mind.

4. If you notice your mind wandering or lost in thought, don't worry. Simply acknowledge the distraction and gently return to the mantra, repeating it again in your mind.

5. Keep repeating the mantra for 10-15 minutes, maintaining an open, nonjudgmental attitude toward the

experience. Try not to get attached to any thoughts or feelings you may experience during meditation.

6. At the end of the allotted time, slowly stop repeating the mantra and sit with your eyes closed for a couple of minutes, allowing your mind and body to absorb the experience of meditation. When you feel ready, open your eyes and return to your daily routine with a sense of renewed peace and tranquility.

Remember that this exercise is only an introduction to Transcendental Meditation and is not a substitute for learning the technique from a qualified teacher. However, it can be useful for experiencing some of the benefits of mantra-based meditation and for getting closer to the practice of transcendental meditation.

CHAPTER 10: METTA MEDITATION: DEVELOPING LOVE AND COMPASSION

Metta meditation, also known as loving-kindness meditation, is a Buddhist practice that is meant to cultivate feelings of love, compassion, empathetic joy, and equanimity toward oneself and others. This practice helps to develop an attitude of benevolence and openness towards all forms of life and to overcome barriers such as anger, fear and judgment.

The goal of metta meditation is to expand our hearts and minds to accommodate all sentient beings, without distinction or preference. Here's how to practice metta meditation:

1. Find a quiet, comfortable place to sit in a position that allows you to keep your back straight and your body relaxed. Close your eyes and take a few moments to bring attention to your breath and body.

2. Start by cultivating loving-kindness toward yourself. Silently repeat phrases such as "May I be happy", "May I be at peace", "May I be healthy" and "May I live with ease" in your mind. Let these words resonate in your heart

and mind, generating a sense of love and compassion for yourself.

3. Next, extend these feelings of loving-kindness to a loved one, such as a friend, family member, or partner. Visualize this person in your mind and repeat the same phrases, replacing "I" with the person's noun or pronoun: "May you be happy", "May you be at peace", etc. Feel how your heart expands with love and compassion for this person.

4. Continue to expand your circle of loving-kindness by including other people in your practice: acquaintances, colleagues, neighbors, and even people with whom you may have difficulty or conflict. Try to maintain an open and welcoming attitude towards everyone, regardless of your personal relationships with them.

5. Finally, extend your metta practice to all sentient beings, regardless of species, race, religion, or condition. Repeat phrases such as "May all beings be happy," "May all beings be at peace," "May all beings be healthy," and "May all beings live with ease." Let your heart expand further, embracing the entire universe in love and compassion.

6. After practicing metta meditation for about 10-15 minutes, bring your attention back to your breath and body. Take a few moments to integrate the experience and then, when you feel ready, open your eyes and go back to your daily life, taking with you the sense of love and compassion you cultivated during your practice.

Metta meditation, or loving-kindness meditation, is a practice deeply rooted in the Theravada Buddhist tradition, especially in the Vipassana schools of meditation. This practice is meant to cultivate and nurture feelings of unconditional love, compassion, sympathy and acceptance towards oneself, others and all sentient beings.

The importance of metta meditation has been emphasized by

many Buddhist teachers, including the Dalai Lama, who affirm that love and compassion are the foundations for true peace and harmony in the world. The practice of metta meditation can help dissolve the barriers of prejudice, hatred and fear that often divide people and cultures, fostering a sense of interconnectedness and oneness among all living beings.

Metta meditation is more than just a meditation technique; it is a way of living and perceiving the world around us. By practicing metta meditation regularly, we learn to develop an attitude of loving-kindness and compassion in every aspect of our lives, from our relationship with ourselves and with others, to our relationship with our environment and social issues.

One of the key aspects of metta meditation is the focus on equanimity, which means maintaining an open and loving heart towards all beings, regardless of our personal preferences, likes or dislikes. Equanimity helps us to overcome attachment and aversion, two of the main causes of suffering in Buddhist philosophy, and to recognize our common humanity and vulnerability.

Another important aspect of metta meditation is its inclusive and universal nature. While other forms of meditation, such as mindfulness meditation or transcendental meditation, focus primarily on the individual and one's mind, metta meditation encourages us to expand our hearts and minds to include all sentient beings, without discrimination or partiality.

Many scientific studies have demonstrated the benefits of metta meditation, including reducing stress, increasing emotional resilience, improving interpersonal relationships, and lowering blood pressure. Additionally, the practice of metta meditation can help develop greater empathy and understanding for others, helping us to become more loving, compassionate, and mindful people.

In conclusion, metta meditation is a powerful and transformative practice that can bring about profound changes in our lives and the world around us. Through the habit of cultivating loving-kindness and compassion, we can transform our minds, hearts, and relationships with others.

The practice of metta meditation teaches us to welcome every experience and every individual with love, understanding and acceptance, helping to create a more peaceful and harmonious world for all.

To further delve into the practice of metta meditation, you can follow a few steps:

1. Study Buddhist teachings on loving-kindness and compassion, as well as the works of contemporary masters such as Thich Nhat Hanh, Jack Kornfield and Sharon Salzberg.

2. Attend metta meditation courses or retreats, where you can learn and practice under the guidance of expert teachers.

3. Integrate metta meditation practice with other forms of meditation and spiritual development, such as mindfulness meditation, Vipassana meditation, and Zen meditation.

4. Cultivate the practice of metta in daily life, seeking to maintain an attitude of loving kindness and compassion towards oneself and others at all times and situations.

5. Share your metta meditation practice with others, encouraging friends and family to try this powerful form of meditation and to discuss your experiences and progress.

6. Support organizations and initiatives that promote loving-kindness, compassion and understanding between different cultures, religions and communities.

The practice of metta meditation can be a path of personal and collective transformation, benefiting not only ourselves, but also all the people and beings we meet on our journey. Through dedication and unwavering commitment to the practice of loving-kindness, we can help create a more loving, compassionate, and united world.

Remember that metta meditation is not just a formal practice, but a lifestyle and attitude that we can carry with us into every moment of our day. Try to cultivate loving-kindness in your relationships with others, in your daily activities, and in the way you think about yourself and the world around you.

Through the practice of metta meditation, it is possible to transform our minds and hearts, helping to create a more loving and compassionate world for all.

Practice Exercise To start practicing metta meditation, follow these simple steps:

1. Find a quiet, distraction-free place where you can meditate. Sit comfortably in a chair or cushion, with your back straight but relaxed.

2. Close your eyes and pay attention to your breathing. Observe the natural flow of air flowing in and out of your nostrils, without trying to change or control it.

3. After a few minutes of focusing on your breathing, begin reciting a few sentences of loving-kindness in your mind. These phrases can vary depending on your preferences, but a common example is: "May I be happy, may I be at peace, may I be healthy, may I live with ease".

4. Repeat these phrases in your mind for a few minutes, focusing on their meaning and your desire to develop love and compassion for yourself.

5. Now expand your field of loving-kindness to include

other people or beings. You can start with the people closest to you, such as family and friends, and then extend your practice to acquaintances, strangers, and finally all sentient beings. For each person or group of people, mentally recite phrases similar to those used for yourself, for example: "May you be happy, may you be at peace, may you be healthy, may you live with ease." .

6. During this stage of metta meditation, it is important to maintain an attitude of equanimity, seeking to cultivate feelings of love and compassion for all people, regardless of their actions or your relationship with them.

7. After you have extended your metta practice to all sentient beings, take a moment to reflect on your experience and the feelings of love, compassion, and interconnectedness you have developed.

8. Finally, close the metta meditation by bringing your attention back to your breathing for a few minutes, before reopening your eyes and returning to your daily life.

The practice of metta meditation can be done daily or integrated into other forms of meditation. With time and regular practice, you will notice a profound change in how you perceive yourself, others and the world around you, developing a more open, loving and compassionate heart.

CHAPTER 11: EXERCISE BREATHING MEDITATION: REGAINING INNER BALANCE

Breathing meditation is one of the simplest and most effective meditative techniques to find inner balance and re-establish the connection with our body and mind. This practice, also known as Anapanasati in Buddhism, involves focusing attention on the breath and using it as an anchor to stay present and aware of the present moment.

Breathing meditation offers many benefits, including:

1. Reducing Stress and Anxiety: By focusing on your breath, you can calm your mind and relieve symptoms of stress and anxiety.

2. Improved Focus and Memory: Regular practice of breathing meditation can increase your ability to focus and improve cognitive function.

3. Promoting Relaxation and Overall Well-Being: Breathing

meditation helps relax the body and mind, promotes better sleep, and contributes to a sense of overall well-being.

4. Developing Self-Awareness and Intuition: Breath meditation can help you develop greater awareness of your emotions, thoughts, and bodily sensations, increasing your ability to understand and handle difficult situations.

Breathing meditation is one of the oldest and most widespread meditative techniques, belonging to the Buddhist tradition, but also present in other cultures and spiritual practices. It relies on awareness of the breath to help calm the mind and bring attention to the present moment. Below are some insights into breathing meditation and how it can be used to improve mental and emotional well-being.

One of the reasons breath meditation is so effective is that the breath is always present and available as an object of attention. Unlike other techniques that require the use of mental imagery or external sounds, breathing meditation can be practiced anytime, anywhere. Also, focusing on your breath helps take your attention away from thoughts and worries that can create stress and anxiety.

Breath meditation can be practiced in a variety of positions, including sitting, lying down, or even standing. The important thing is to maintain a comfortable and relaxed posture that allows you to breathe freely and effortlessly. As you begin to meditate, you may find it helpful to close your eyes to reduce visual distractions and make it easier to focus on your breath.

During breathing meditation, it is common for the mind to wander or get lost in thought. When this happens, the goal is to simply notice the distraction and, without judgment or frustration, gently bring your attention back to your breath. With practice, it will become easier to maintain attention on the breath and develop greater awareness of the present moment.

Breathing meditation can be practiced for any length of time, although experts recommend starting with short sessions of 5 to 10 minutes a day and gradually increasing the duration as it becomes easier to maintain attention. It is important to be patient and kind to yourself during your practice, as meditation is a skill that takes time and effort to develop.

Finally, breathing meditation can be enriched with the use of complementary techniques, such as body scan, which involves mindfully observing physical sensations throughout the body, or metta meditation, which focuses on developing love and compassion for themselves and for others others. Integrating these techniques can help you deepen your meditation practice further and achieve greater benefits.

Practical exercise for breathing meditation:

1. Find a quiet place where you won't be disturbed and get into a comfortable position, sitting or lying down. Make sure your back is straight but relaxed and your head is well supported.

2. Close your eyes to eliminate visual distractions and pay attention to your breathing. Notice the physical sensations associated with inhaling and exhaling, such as cool air entering your nostrils and warm air leaving.

3. Without trying to control your breath, just observe it curiously and without judgment. If your mind begins to wander, acknowledge the thoughts and gently bring your attention back to your breath.

4. If you like, you can count your breaths to help you stay focused. For example, count "one" as you inhale and "two" as you exhale, continuing to ten and then starting over.

5. Continue to practice breathing meditation for at least

5-10 minutes, trying to keep your attention focused on the sensations of the breath and gently pushing away any thoughts or worries.

6. Conclude the meditation by slowly bringing your attention back to your surroundings, listening to the sounds and feeling the temperature of the air against your skin. When you feel ready, open your eyes and take a moment to reflect on the experience.

Regular practice of breathing meditation can lead to increased awareness of the present moment, reduction of stress and anxiety, and a sense of inner peace and well-being. Remember that meditation is a skill that takes time and effort to develop, so be patient and kind to yourself in the process.

Breathing meditation can be practiced daily or integrated into other forms of meditation and spiritual development. With regular practice, you'll discover greater self-awareness, a calmer mind, and a sense of inner balance that will help you better manage the stresses and challenges of everyday life.

Importantly, meditation is a process and it can take time and patience to develop the ability to keep your attention on your breath and to let go of thoughts and distractions. Therefore, it is essential to be kind and patient with yourself during the practice and not to get discouraged if the results are not immediate.

A helpful tip for those who find it difficult to focus on the breath is to use a "mantra" or word of focus that can be repeated mentally as you inhale and exhale. For example, you could mentally repeat "I inhale" as you inhale and "I exhale" as you exhale. This helps maintain attention and reduce the tendency of the mind to wander.

Also, if you find your mind is particularly restless or full of thoughts, you could try practicing a guided meditation, in which a teacher or recording guides you through the process of focusing on your breath and relaxing your body and mind.

Remember that meditation is a personal tool and that it is important to find the method that works best for you. Experiment with different techniques and approaches until you find one that helps you achieve a sense of balance and inner well-being.

In conclusion, breathing meditation is a simple yet powerful practice that can offer numerous benefits for the mind, body and spirit. Take time each day to cultivate this skill, and you'll soon discover a sense of peace and balance that will permeate all aspects of your life.

CHAPTER 12: WALKING MEDITATION: AWARENESS IN MOTION

Walking meditation, also known as "kinhin" in the Zen tradition, is a form of moving meditation that integrates awareness of the body and mind with the act of walking. This practice offers an alternative to sitting meditation, allowing you to cultivate mindfulness and awareness even during physical activity.

Meditating while walking can be especially helpful for those who find it difficult to stay still for long periods or who want to integrate meditation into their daily routine. Walking meditation is also a great way to take a mental break and relax during a stressful day.

Here is a step-by-step guide to practicing walking meditation:

1. Find a suitable location: Look for a quiet, safe outdoor space where you can walk without distractions, such as a park or garden. If you can't practice outdoors, choose a large, unobstructed indoor space.

2. Mentally Prepare: Before you begin, take a moment to relax

your mind and body. Take a few deep breaths and bring your attention to the present moment.

3. Start Walking: Advance slowly with a natural, balanced stride. Be aware of the contact of the feet with the ground, the movement of the legs and arms, and the posture of the body.

4. Bring your attention to your breath: As you walk, focus your attention on your breath, noticing how it synchronizes with the rhythm of your steps. If your mind begins to wander, gently bring your focus back to your breath and body movement.

5. Observe the world around you: As you practice walking meditation, pay attention to the sounds, smells, and sensations you encounter along the way. Try to remain open and curious, welcoming each experience without judgment.

6. Conclude the practice: After walking for at least 10-15 minutes, slow down and return to a still point. Take a moment to reflect on the experience and how you are feeling physically and mentally.

Walking meditation can be a wonderful way to integrate your meditation practice into your daily life and to connect with the world around you. This type of meditation offers a number of benefits, including stress reduction, improved focus, and an increased sense of well-being.

Additionally, walking meditation can be tailored to your personal needs, allowing you to practice at different paces and intensities. Some practitioners prefer to walk slowly and silently, while others choose a more energetic and vigorous pace. The important thing is to find an approach that works for you and that helps you cultivate awareness and mindfulness.

With time and regular practice, walking meditation can become a natural part of your daily routine, providing you with an opportunity to reconnect with yourself and your surroundings. Experiment with different techniques and find the one that resonates with you the most, so you can get the most benefit from this age-old practice.

As you continue to practice walking meditation, you may find that your present-moment awareness deepens and that your ability to manage stress and daily struggles improves.

Additionally, walking meditation can help you develop greater gratitude for the beauty and simplicity of life.

For those who wish to delve further into the practice of walking meditation, there are several traditions and teachings that offer a wide variety of approaches and methods.

For example, the Theravada Buddhist tradition proposes a practice called "Cankama", which consists of walking back and forth along a pre-established path, focusing on awareness of the body and mind.

Similarly, in the Japanese Zen tradition, "Kinhin" walking meditation is often practiced as a complement to sitting meditation, providing an opportunity to invigorate the body and mind between meditation sessions.

If you'd like to integrate other forms of moving meditation into your practice, you might also consider disciplines like Tai Chi or Qigong, which combine fluid, mindful movement with deep breathing and mental relaxation.

Ultimately, walking meditation presents a unique opportunity to cultivate awareness and mindfulness in the context of daily activities.
Through regular practice, you will discover a greater ability to manage stress, to connect with yourself and the world around you, and ultimately to live a more balanced and fulfilling life.

Remember that, as with all forms of meditation, the key to success lies in persistence and dedication to practice, which will allow you to reap the long-term benefits of walking meditation.

Practical exercise for walking meditation:

1. Find a quiet, safe space where you can practice walking meditation, both indoors and outdoors.
2. Begin walking slowly, focusing on the movement of your body and the contact of your feet with the ground.
3. Notice the rhythm of your breathing and how it syncs with your steps.
4. Observe your surroundings with curiosity and without judgment.
5. Practice walking meditation for at least 10-15 minutes, concluding with a moment to reflect on your experience.

CHAPTER 13: MEDITATION ON VISUALIZATIONS: CREATING POSITIVE MENTAL IMAGES

Visualization meditation is a technique of using the mind to create specific, positive mental images to promote well-being, healing, and personal development. This type of meditation can be especially helpful for those who have difficulty focusing on their breathing or a mantra, as the use of mental imagery can help focus and immerse you in your meditation practice.

Visualizations can be of various types, depending on the goals and personal preferences of the practitioner. For example, you might imagine relaxing natural landscapes, such as a beach or forest, or specific situations, such as meeting a loved one or accomplishing a personal goal. Visualizations can also be more abstract, such as creating a mental picture of positive energy flowing through the body and taking away stress and tension.

Visualization meditation is an ancient practice used in many cultures and spiritual traditions to cultivate the mind and promote physical, emotional, and spiritual well-being. This form of meditation is based on using the mind to create positive and vivid mental images in order to influence external reality and our internal state.

Visualizations can be used to relax, reduce stress, increase focus, improve self-esteem, promote healing, and achieve personal or spiritual goals.

Visualizations can take many different forms, depending on individual preferences and goals. For example, you might imagine that you are in a quiet, relaxing place, such as a beach or a garden, and you are absorbing the positive, calming energy of the environment. Similarly, you might visualize yourself being successful or accomplishing an important goal, and feel the positive emotions associated with that success.

To begin a visualization meditation, find a quiet, distraction-free place. Sit comfortably, close your eyes and take a few deep, slow breaths, allowing your body and mind to relax. Once you feel relaxed, start creating a mental picture in your mind. Try to make the image as vivid and detailed as possible, involving all the senses: sight, hearing, smell, taste and touch.

As you visualize the image, try to keep your mind focused and present, not letting your thoughts wander. If you notice your mind wandering, simply acknowledge the thought and gently bring your attention back to the image you are viewing.

Once you have finished your visualization meditation, take a few minutes to reflect on the experience and how you are feeling. Notice any changes in your mood, thoughts, or physical sensations.

Here is a practical visualization exercise you can try:

1. Sit comfortably in a relaxed position and close your eyes.
2. Take a few deep, slow breaths, letting your body and mind relax.

3. Imagine yourself in a beautiful and lush garden, full of colorful and fragrant flowers.
4. As you slowly move through the garden, you feel the soft grass under your feet and the warmth of the sun on your skin.
5. Listen to the gentle sound of flowing water in a nearby fountain and birdsong in the trees.
6. Inhale deeply and smell the flowers around you.
7. Approach the fountain and watch as the water gently glides over the stones, creating a soothing and calming sound.
8. Take a sip of this fresh, pure water, feeling how it flows through your body, bringing well-being and healing to every cell.
9. As you continue to explore the garden, imagine that every flower you touch gives you a feeling of love, compassion, and gratitude. Let these emotions fill and envelop you completely.
10. Spend a few minutes in this rejuvenating garden, absorbing all the positive feelings and healing energy it offers.
11. When you're ready, slowly bring your attention to your breathing and start sensing your body and the room you're in.
12. Take one last deep breath and open your eyes, taking with you the feeling of peace and renewal you experienced in the garden.

By practicing this regularly visualization exercise, you may notice an improvement in your ability to relax and manage everyday stress and tension. Additionally, practicing visualization can help you develop your creativity, your intuition, and your ability to manifest your desires and goals in real life.

Remember that visualization meditation is an art that requires constant effort and practice. Don't be discouraged if you can't create sharp, detailed mental images right from the start, or if your mind tends to wander during the exercise. With practice and patience, you will find that your visualization skills will grow stronger and more powerful, bringing remarkable benefits to your life.

In summary, visualization meditation offers an effective and rewarding way to cultivate the mind and promote physical, emotional, and spiritual well-being. Experiment with different visualization techniques to find out which ones work best for you, and incorporate these practices into your daily routine for maximum benefits.

CHAPTER 14: MEDITATION ON MANDALAS: THE UNIVERSE IN A CIRCLE

Mandalas, which mean "circle" in Sanskrit, are symbolic representations of the universe used in various spiritual traditions, especially Buddhism and Hinduism. These intricate, geometric artworks are often used as meditation tools to help focus attention, calm the mind, and promote spiritual awareness.

Mandalas are symbolic diagrams used in various spiritual and cultural traditions, including Buddhism and Hinduism. The word "mandala" comes from Sanskrit and means "circle". Mandalas are characterized by geometric, symmetrical and circular shapes that represent the universe and its energies. They are used as meditation tools, to aid concentration and promote relaxation, healing and spiritual growth.

The origins of mandalas date back thousands of years, when they were used in religious rites and as architectural decorations. Over the centuries, mandalas have taken on a deeper and more symbolic meaning and have become tools for meditation and self-exploration.

Mandalas can be created using a variety of materials and techniques, including painting, drawing and sculpting. Tibetan mandalas, for example, are often created using colored sand and then destroyed as a symbol of impermanence.

Other mandalas can be painted on canvas, engraved on metal or carved in stone.

Each mandala is unique and reflects the symbolism and spirituality of the culture and tradition it comes from. Mandalas can include images of deities, animals and human figures, as well as complex geometric shapes and intricate floral designs. The colors used in mandalas can also have symbolic and spiritual meaning.

Mandala meditation is a practice involving concentration and visualization, with the aim of achieving a state of calm and inner awareness. Mandala meditation is believed to help balance physical, mental, and emotional energies, promoting healing and personal transformation.

The practice of meditating on mandalas can offer a number of benefits, including:

1. Stress and Anxiety Reduction: The concentration required in mandala meditation helps to calm the mind and take it away from negative and worrisome thoughts.

2. Improved concentration and memory: Regular practice of mandala meditation can help develop greater concentration and awareness, which in turn can improve memory and learning ability.

3. Developing intuition and creativity: Meditation on mandalas can stimulate imagination and creativity, allowing you to explore your inner world and discover new insights and ideas.

4. Energetic and spiritual balance: Mandalas represent the

universe and its energies, and meditating on them can help balance and harmonize the energies of body and spirit.

5. Connectivity with the Higher Self: Meditating on mandalas can facilitate connection with the higher self and promote spiritual growth. Through this practice, one can access greater inner wisdom and spiritual guidance.

Meditating on mandalas can be an effective way to develop focus, calm the mind, and connect to a sense of oneness with the universe.

Here is a practical mandala meditation exercise you can try:

1. Choose a mandala that you like and that inspires you. You can use a printed image, a mandala book, or even a digital mandala on your electronic device. Make sure the image is large enough that you can see it clearly, but not so large that it is distracted by the details.

2. Find a quiet, comfortable place to sit for meditation. Make sure you have good posture, with a straight back and feet planted firmly on the ground. If you prefer, you can also sit on a pillow or folded blanket for extra support.

3. Take a few minutes to relax your body and mind, focusing on your breathing. Inhale slowly and deeply, and then exhale slowly and completely. Keep breathing like this until you feel calm and centered.

4. Gaze into the center of the mandala, allowing your peripheral vision to perceive the entire design. As you do this, try not to focus on any specific detail of the mandala, but rather let your mind immerse yourself in the whole of the image.

5. As you continue to gaze at the center of the mandala, allow your mind to become increasingly still and silent. If you notice your mind starting to wander, simply gently bring your attention back to the center of the mandala.

6. Continue meditating on the mandala for any length of time that feels appropriate to you, which could be anywhere from 10 minutes to an hour or more. During this time, try to maintain a state of calm and focus, allowing any thought or emotion to arise and pass without judgment.

7. When you feel the time is right, slowly bring your attention to your breathing and start sensing your body and the room you are in. Take one last deep breath and open your eyes, taking with you the feeling of peace and focus you experienced during meditation.

Practicing mandala meditation regularly can lead to a number of benefits, including increased focus, increased self-awareness, and a greater connection to the world around you. Additionally, mandala meditation can help reduce stress, enhance creativity, and develop patience.

As you practice mandala meditation, you may find that your concentration and mindfulness skills improve dramatically. You may also notice that you become more open and receptive to everyday life experiences, and that you are able to deal with stressful situations with greater calmness and clarity.

It is important to remember that the practice of mandala meditation, like any other form of meditation, takes time and dedication. Don't be discouraged if you don't notice immediate improvements—the key is constant practice and a desire to develop your inner awareness.

Finally, don't be afraid to experiment with different mandalas in your meditation practice. Each mandala has a unique energy and can lead to different meditative experiences. Find one that resonates with you and helps you achieve a state of focus and inner peace.

In conclusion, mandala meditation is an ancient and powerful practice that can offer numerous benefits for the mind, body and spirit. Through regular practice and a desire to develop mindfulness, it is possible to achieve a sense of balance and oneness with the universe around us.

CHAPTER 15: MEDITATION SOUNDS AND MANTRAS: THE POWER OF VIBRATIONS

Sound and mantra meditation is based on the use of repetitive sounds, words and phrases to focus the mind and achieve a state of deep relaxation. This practice is rooted in the ancient spiritual traditions of India and Tibet, but has also been adopted by many other cultures and meditation traditions over the centuries.

Mantras are sacred words, phrases, or sounds that are repeated during meditation with the intent to help the mind focus and enter a state of calm and awareness. Originally derived from the Hindu and Buddhist tradition, mantras are now used in different forms of meditation and spiritual practices around the world.

Mantras can be composed of words or phrases in Sanskrit, an ancient language of India, or of specific sounds believed to have a particular spiritual or vibrational meaning. An example of a well-known Sanskrit mantra is "Om", which represents universal energy and creation.

Other examples of Sanskrit mantras include "Om mani padme hum", which means "the jewel in the heart of the lotus" and "Om namo bhagavate vasudevaya", which means "obeisance to the Lord who resides in all beings".

Mantras are not limited to the Sanskrit language; they can also be meaningful words or phrases in any language that help focus the mind and create an atmosphere of calm and collectedness.

For example, you might choose a mantra in English or another language that speaks to you, such as "peace," "love," or "gratitude." The repetition of the mantra during meditation serves to focus the mind, preventing thoughts from wandering and allowing the practitioner to reach a state of calm and awareness.

Mantras can be repeated mentally, whispered or chanted aloud, depending on personal preferences and specific traditions. Repetition of the mantra may be accompanied by counting on a mala, a rosary-like beaded necklace, to help maintain focus and mark progression through practice.

In addition to the immediate benefits of calming the mind and facilitating concentration, regular mantra practice is believed to have long-term beneficial effects on mental, emotional and spiritual health. Mantras can help reduce stress, increase self-esteem and self-awareness, and promote a sense of well-being and inner harmony.

In conclusion, mantras are a central element of many meditative and spiritual practices and offer an effective way to focus the mind and promote a state of calmness and awareness. Experiment with different mantras and find out which ones work best for you, engaging in regular practice to experience the many benefits that mantra meditation can offer.

Here are some of the benefits of meditation sounds and mantras:

1. Improves Concentration and Focus: Repetition

of mantras helps keep the mind focused and focused, reducing destructive thoughts and promoting mental clarity.

2. Reduces Stress and Anxiety: Meditation sounds and mantras can help relax the body and mind, relieving stress and anxiety and promoting a sense of calm and well-being.

3. Promotes Healing: The vibrations produced by mantras are believed to have the ability to stimulate healing at a cellular level, improving physical and mental health.

4. Promotes Spiritual Growth: Regular practice of sound and mantra meditation can help you develop greater self-awareness and a deeper connection with the divine or your own spirituality.

Practical exercise:

1. Choose a Mantra: Choose a mantra that has a particular meaning to you or that resonates with your meditation intentions. Some common mantras include "Om", "So-ham" and "Om mani padme hum".

2. Find a quiet place: Look for a quiet and comfortable place to practice meditation, away from distractions and noise.

3. Sit comfortably: Sit in a comfortable position, with your back straight and your hands on your knees or thighs. Close your eyes and relax your body and mind.

4. Breathe deeply: Before you begin chanting the mantra, take a few deep, slow breaths, focusing on the sensation of the air moving in and out of your body.

5. Recite the mantra: Start reciting the mantra mentally or aloud, focusing all your attention on the sound and meaning of the words. Repeat the mantra for at least 10-15 minutes, or longer if you wish.

6. Conclude the Meditation: When you feel ready, stop chanting the mantra and be silent for a few minutes, allowing your mind to absorb the energy and vibrations created during the meditation. Take a few deep, slow breaths, and when you feel ready, open your eyes and slowly return to your normal awareness.

Practicing sound and mantra meditation regularly can bring many benefits, including better mental and emotional balance, increased self-awareness, and a deeper connection to your spirituality. Remember that the key to an effective meditation practice is consistency, so try to commit to meditating every day, even if it's just for a few minutes.

As you become more comfortable with meditation sounds and mantras, you may want to explore other meditation techniques or combine this practice with other forms of meditation, such as walking meditation or mindfulness breathing meditation. The important thing is to find a practice that helps you achieve a state of inner peace and general well-being.

In conclusion, sound and mantra meditation is a powerful and versatile practice that can improve your life in many ways. Experiment with different mantras and meditation techniques to find out which one works best for you, and keep cultivating your practice to experience the lasting benefits of meditation.

CHAPTER 16: YOGA NIDRA MEDITATION: MINDFUL SLEEP

Yoga Nidra, also known as mindful sleep or yogi's sleep, is a deeply relaxing meditation technique that brings the practitioner into a state of consciousness between wakefulness and sleep. This practice has roots in the ancient traditions of yoga and the Himalayas and has been developed and adapted for use in the modern context. Yoga Nidra can help reduce stress, improve sleep, promote healing, and support overall well-being.

Yoga Nidra, also known as "mindful sleep" or "yogic sleep," is a deep meditation practice that combines relaxation, mindfulness, and intention to help rebalance the mind and body. This form of meditation was developed in ancient India and is based on traditional yoga techniques, such as pratyahara (withdrawal of the senses) and dharana (concentration).

In Yoga Nidra, one enters a state of deep, yet mindful relaxation, which is similar to the half-awake state between sleep and wakefulness.

During practice, you are guided through several stages, which may include:

1. Body relaxation: It begins with muscle relaxation exercises and deep breathing to help release physical and mental tension.

2. Relaxation of the senses: We then move on to the withdrawal of the senses, focusing on listening to internal and external sounds and observing bodily sensations.

3. Intention (Sankalpa): An intention or positive affirmation is set for the practice, which helps focus the mind and promote personal change.

4. Awareness Rotation: Moves awareness through different parts of the body, further relaxing each area and increasing body awareness.

5. Visualizations: You can be guided through a series of mental visualizations, such as images of natural landscapes, symbols or situations, to stimulate the imagination and promote awareness.

6. Breath awareness: Focus attention on the breath, observing the natural flow of incoming and outgoing air.

7. Reconnecting with Intention: One returns to the intention or affirmation established at the beginning of the practice, reinforcing its meaning and impact.

8. Return to ordinary consciousness: Gradually, one comes out of the state of deep relaxation and returns to ordinary consciousness, bringing with it a feeling of renewed balance and well-being.

The benefits of Yoga Nidra are numerous and can include reducing stress, improving sleep, developing self-awareness, and strengthening the mind-body connection.

However, as with any meditation practice, it's important to be patient and persevere, as results can vary from person to person and can take time to manifest.

The practice of Yoga Nidra usually begins with the practitioner lying on their back in a comfortable position, with eyes closed and the body completely relaxed. It may be helpful to use a pillow under your head or knees to support your spine and ensure maximum comfort while practicing. Your surroundings should be quiet and comfortable, with a pleasant temperature and dim light.

Once the practitioner is settled and relaxed, the guided Yoga Nidra meditation can begin. The Yoga Nidra process usually includes several stages, such as relaxing the body, awareness of the breath, and focusing on specific physical sensations or mental images. During the practice, it is important to remain in a state of deep relaxation, without falling asleep completely.

In-depth practical exercise:

1. Find a quiet, comfortable place to lie down, making sure your body is well supported and relaxed.
2. Close your eyes and bring your attention to your breath, noticing how it goes in and out of your body.
3. Begin to relax your body, starting at your feet and slowly working your way up to your head. With each exhalation, imagine yourself releasing tension and stress.
4. Once your body is completely relaxed, bring your attention to your forehead. Imagine a warm and relaxing light spreading from the forehead to the whole body.
5. Now, imagine that you are in a safe and peaceful place, such as a beach or a garden. Absorb the sensory details of this place, such as the sounds, smells and sensations on the skin.
6. Visualize a bright light in the center of your chest, a symbol of love and compassion. Imagine this light expanding, filling your entire body and radiating out into

the world around you.

7. Bring your attention to your breath and slowly begin to bring your awareness back to your body and surroundings. Slowly wiggle your fingers and toes, and when you feel ready, open your eyes.

8. Take a few moments to reflect on the Yoga Nidra experience and how you feel after the practice. Remember that each Yoga Nidra session can be different and that it is normal for thoughts and feelings to change over time.

Regular practice of Yoga Nidra can offer a number of benefits, including increased self-awareness, better stress management, and more restful sleep.

However, it's important to remember that Yoga Nidra is just one of many meditation techniques available and that it may not be suitable for everyone. If you are interested in further exploring Yoga Nidra or other meditation techniques, consider working with an experienced teacher or joining a meditation class or retreat to deepen your practice and receive personalized guidance.

CHAPTER 17: MEDITATION AND CREATIVITY: THE ENCOUNTER BETWEEN ART AND SILENCE

Meditation and creativity are often thought of as two distinct worlds, but in reality they are deeply interconnected. Meditation can help clear your mind of everyday worries and enter a state of greater awareness, openness, and creative flow. In this chapter, we will explore how meditation can enhance creativity and how meditative techniques can be integrated into artistic practices.

1. Open your mind: Meditation helps us clear our minds of distractions and enter a state of relaxation and openness. When the mind is free from worries, it is easier to access the source of creativity and find inspiration.

2. Develop Attention: Meditation teaches us to focus attention and observe our thoughts without judgment.

This skill of concentration can be applied to art, helping us to fully immerse ourselves in the creative process and perceive the finer details.

3. Cultivate mindfulness: Meditation encourages us to be present and aware of the moment. This awareness can help us see things from different perspectives and discover new ideas and creative solutions.

The encounter between art and silence is a fundamental aspect in the creative process. Both can be seen as tools to explore our inner selves, connect with ourselves, and shape our deepest emotions and thoughts. In this sense, art and silence can work together to create an experience of personal growth and self-expression.

Silence is often underestimated in our modern society, characterized by constant noise and stimuli. However, silence can have a profound impact on our creativity and emotional well-being. In silence, we can hear our inner voice and give space to our deepest ideas and intuitions.

Art, in turn, is a way of giving shape to these ideas and intuitions, allowing us to express and communicate what we feel and perceive in our inner world. Art can be a bridge between silence and the outside world, a way to bring to light what would otherwise remain hidden.

When we combine art and silence through meditation, we can create a fertile environment for personal growth and the discovery of new perspectives and inspirations.

Meditation allows us to immerse ourselves in silence and tune in to our creativity, providing us with a unique opportunity to explore our inner world and shape our ideas.

Here are some ways to deepen the encounter between art and silence in your meditation practice:

1. Set aside time each day for silent meditation. Even just a few minutes of silence can have a significant impact on your creativity and emotional well-being.

2. Experiment with different forms of meditation, such as walking meditation, meditating on a picture or artwork, or meditating to music. These techniques can help you connect with your creativity in different and inspiring ways.

3. Create a space dedicated to meditation and art in your home or studio. This space should be quiet and free from distractions, where you can immerse yourself in silence and focus on your art practice.

4. Attend meditation and art workshops or retreats, where you can explore the encounter between art and silence in an environment of support and inspiration.

5. Reflect on how silence and art affect your daily life and try to integrate these experiences into your routine and your relationships with others.

Ultimately, the encounter between art and silence can lead to greater awareness, creativity and emotional well-being. By incorporating silence and art into your meditation practice, you will be able to discover new sources of inspiration and develop a deeper and more authentic approach to self-expression and creativity.

Practical exercise: Meditation for creativity

1. Find a quiet, comfortable place to sit or lie down. Make sure you are free from distractions for at least 15-20 minutes.

2. Close your eyes and start focusing on your breathing. Observe the natural flow of air as it enters and exits your

nostrils. Don't try to control your breath, but allow it to flow freely and effortlessly.

3. After a few minutes, imagine yourself in a serene and inspiring place. It could be a deserted beach, a lush forest or a flower garden. Feel the sounds, smells and sensations of this place and allow your mind to fully immerse yourself in the environment.

4. While in this space, imagine having at your disposal all the tools and materials you need to create a work of art. This can be brushes and paints, musical instruments, sculpting materials, or anything else you can think of.

5. Let your mind freely explore the creative possibilities and start imagining the work of art you would like to create. Don't judge your ideas or worry about the outcome; just allow your creativity to flow freely.

6. After spending time imagining and "creating" in your meditative space, bring your attention back to your breathing. Take a few minutes to breathe out and slowly come back to reality.

7. When you feel ready, open your eyes and take a moment to reflect on the experience. If you like, jot down any ideas or images that came to your mind during the meditation.

8. Over the next few days, try to integrate these ideas into your art practice. You may find that meditation has helped you unlock new ideas and find greater inspiration.

By repeating this exercise regularly, you can deepen your connection with art and silence and develop a meditative practice that nurtures your creativity and emotional well-being.

In conclusion, meditation and creativity are closely linked and can support each other in the process of self-expression and personal growth. By integrating meditation into your art practice, you can discover new ideas, deepen your awareness, and experience the pleasure of creative flow.

CHAPTER 18: MEDITATION AND SPORTS: IMPROVING PHYSICAL AND MENTAL PERFORMANCE

Meditation can have a significant impact on sports performance, both physically and mentally. Many elite athletes use meditation as an integral part of their training, to improve concentration, manage stress and develop greater mental resilience.

Meditation helps athletes develop greater awareness of their bodies and their sensations, allowing them to sense and correct imbalances and tensions before they can turn into injuries. Additionally, meditative practice can help develop greater ability to concentrate and focus, which are critical to success in any sport.

Some of the benefits of meditation in sports include:

1. Stress and Anxiety Reduction: Meditation helps manage the stress and anxiety that can arise from the competition

and pressures of training, promoting relaxation and mental calm.

2. Improved Focus: Meditation can help athletes develop greater focus and maintain concentration during competitions and workouts.

3. Increased Mental Resilience: Meditation can help athletes develop greater mental resilience, enabling them to better cope with the challenges and difficulties that may arise in sport.

4. Performance Enhancement: Meditation can help athletes improve their performance through increased body awareness and better management of emotions and tensions.

To further explore the link between meditation and sport, we'll look at the underlying mechanisms that explain how meditation can improve physical and mental performance.

1. Concentration and mental focus: Meditation helps develop the ability to concentrate and focus the mind. This is especially important in sports, where the focus must be on a specific task, such as hitting a ball, following a game strategy, or keeping pace during a run. Meditation can help athletes stay focused on the present moment, avoiding distractions and negative thoughts that can negatively affect performance.

2. Stress and Anxiety Management: Athletes often face situations of stress and pressure, such as competition, high expectations and fears of failure. Meditation can teach athletes to manage stress and anxiety more effectively, allowing them to remain calm and centered even in the most challenging situations.

3. Recovery and Healing: Meditation can play an important role in the recovery and healing process after a workout

or competition. By promoting relaxation and stress reduction, meditation can help improve sleep quality, speed muscle recovery and reduce the risk of injury.

4. Developing Mental Resilience: Meditation can help develop mental resilience, which is the ability to adapt and overcome challenges and adversity. Athletes who practice meditation can learn to better handle difficulties, such as injuries, defeats and external pressures, and to stay motivated in pursuing their goals.

5. Improved self-awareness: Meditation helps develop a greater sense of self-awareness, which can be helpful for athletes in recognizing their emotions, thoughts, and physical sensations. This increased self-awareness can help athletes better understand their limitations and potential, and make more informed choices about training, nutrition and recovery.

6. Enhance Empathy and Teamwork: Meditation can help athletes develop empathy and mutual understanding, which are important skills for teamwork and building positive relationships with coaches, teammates, and opponents.

In conclusion, meditation offers many benefits to athletes, both physically and mentally. By integrating meditation into their training routine, athletes can enhance their performance, build resilience, and promote greater awareness and overall well-being.

Below, you'll find an in-depth hands-on exercise athletes can use to experience the benefits of meditation.

Practical exercise: Meditation for athletes

1. Find a quiet, distraction-free place where you can practice meditation without interruption. Make sure you are comfortable, sitting or lying down in a relaxed

position.

2. Start focusing on your breath, slowly inhaling and exhaling through your nose. Pay attention to the sensation of the air flowing in and out of your nostrils and the movement of your diaphragm as you breathe.

3. Now, imagine a sporting situation where you often find yourself under pressure or stress, such as an important competition or a crucial moment in the game. Visualize the situation as clearly as possible in your mind, trying to perceive the sounds, smells and physical sensations associated with that moment.

4. As you continue to visualize this situation, bring your attention to the emotions and thoughts that arise. Without judging or trying to change them, just observe these emotions and thoughts as if they were clouds passing in the sky of your mind.

5. When you notice your mind wandering, gently bring your attention back to your breathing and the sporting situation you're visualizing.

6. Now, imagine that you are approaching the situation with calmness, concentration and self-confidence. Visualize yourself successfully overcoming the challenge and achieving your sporting goals.

7. Finally, bring your attention back to your breath, inhaling and exhaling slowly and deeply several times. When you feel ready, open your eyes and return to your daily life with greater awareness and the ability to face sporting challenges with serenity and concentration.

By practicing this meditation exercise regularly, athletes can develop greater resistance to stress, improve their concentration and promote a more balanced and mindful approach to sporting challenges.

By regularly repeating this meditation exercise, you will be able to develop a greater awareness of your physical and mental abilities and, consequently, enhance your sports performance. Meditation can become a powerful training tool that will help you achieve your goals and push your limits in sport.

CHAPTER 19: MEDITATION AND WORK: MANAGING STRESS AND INCREASING PRODUCTIVITY

Meditation can be a powerful tool to help manage stress and increase productivity at work. In an increasingly fast-paced and competitive work environment, it's essential to find ways to keep your balance and focus on your priorities.

Through greater awareness of oneself and one's environment, it is possible to find balance and inner calm even in the most difficult situations. Here's how meditation can help you achieve these goals:

1. Stress Reduction: Meditation helps you focus on the present moment, allowing you to push away stressful thoughts and worries. Regular practice can decrease levels of cortisol, a hormone related to stress, and increase the

production of endorphins, which promote well-being and happiness.

2. Improved Concentration: Meditation encourages focus on a single point of reference, such as the breath or a mantra, thus training the mind to stay focused. This skill can also be applied to work activities, allowing you to complete tasks in a more effective and timely manner.

3. Increased Creativity: Meditation opens the mind to new ideas and perspectives, stimulating lateral thinking and problem-solving skills. This can lead to more innovative and original solutions at work.

4. Improvement of interpersonal relationships: Meditation promotes empathy and understanding of the emotions of others, helping to improve communication and collaboration between colleagues.

5. Development of emotional resilience: meditation helps to develop greater awareness of one's emotions, allowing one to face stressful situations with more calm and lucidity. This emotional resilience can be especially helpful in managing conflict and tension at work.

To make the most of the benefits of meditation at work, it's important to integrate this practice into your daily routine. Set aside time every day to meditate, even if it's just 10-15 minutes, and choose techniques that suit your personal needs and preferences. With time and consistent practice, you may notice an improvement in your ability to manage stress and increase your productivity at work.

The benefits of meditation at work include:

1. Reduction of stress and anxiety
2. Improved concentration and attention
3. Increased creativity and problem solving skills

4. Developing greater emotional resilience
5. Improvement of interpersonal relationships with colleagues and collaborators

Here is a practical and in-depth exercise to integrate meditation into your work life and manage stress and increase productivity.

"Mindfulness" meditation at work:
1. Find a suitable time: Try to find a time of day when you have a few minutes to devote to meditation. It could be during your lunch break, at the start of the day, or before an important meeting.
2. Find a quiet place: Look for a space where you can feel comfortable and not be disturbed. It can be your office, an empty meeting room, or a quiet corner outdoors.
3. Sit comfortably: Sit on a chair or cushion, with your back straight but relaxed. Place your hands on your legs or knees and close your eyes.
4. Focus your attention on your breath: Bring your attention to your breath, without trying to change it in any way. Watch how the air moves in and out of your nostrils, and feel the movement of your diaphragm as you inhale and exhale.
5. When the mind wanders, return to the breath: it is normal for the mind to wander and start thinking about work or personal matters. When you catch these thoughts, don't judge or resist them, just gently bring your attention back to your breath.

6. Expand Awareness: After practicing focusing on your breath for a few minutes, try expanding your awareness to your body and surroundings. Pay attention to physical sensations, such as the contact of the chair with your body, and the sounds around you.
7. Conclude the meditation: after about 10-15 minutes, or when you feel ready, bring your attention back to the breath. Take a few deep breaths, open your eyes and reconnect with your surroundings. Take a moment to reflect on how you feel and what you have learned in meditation.

By practicing this mindfulness meditation exercise regularly at work, you may notice an improvement in your ability to manage stress and increase productivity. Remember that constant practice is the key to long-lasting results and to reap the full benefits of meditation in your working life.

CHAPTER 20: MEDITATION AND RELATIONSHIPS: CULTIVATING EMPATHY AND COMMUNICATION

Meditation can have a significant impact on our interpersonal relationships, helping us cultivate empathy, understanding and more effective communication. In this chapter, we will explore how meditation can improve our relationship skills.

1. Empathy in Meditation: Meditation helps us develop empathy, which is the ability to put ourselves in the shoes of others and understand their emotions and perspectives. The practice of meditation teaches us to listen carefully, not to judge, and to be present with others, thus improving the quality of our interactions.

2. Conscious Communication: Meditation teaches us to be more aware of our words and how we use them. We learn

to speak with kindness, clarity and sincerity, avoiding fueling conflicts or misunderstandings.

3. Managing Emotions: Meditation helps us understand and manage our emotions, allowing us to respond to difficult situations calmly and clearly. This can help us avoid impulsive reactions that can damage our relationships.

4. Cultivate Self-Compassion: Meditation teaches us to have compassion for ourselves, to recognize our limitations, and to accept our imperfections. This allows us to cultivate more authentic and deep relationships with others.

Empathy is the ability to understand and share another person's feelings by putting yourself in their shoes. Compassion, on the other hand, is the quality of feeling a sincere concern for the well-being of others and a desire to alleviate their suffering.

These two qualities are essential for establishing authentic and deep relationships with others.

Practicing metta meditation regularly can lead to several benefits, including:

1. Enhance Understanding of Others: Metta meditation helps us tune in to the emotions and needs of others, making us more aware of what they may be feeling or wanting.

2. Increasing Kindness and Patience: By cultivating loving-kindness, we learn to be kinder and more patient with others, even when faced with difficult situations or people who challenge us.

3. Reducing the tendency to judge: metta meditation encourages us to welcome others as they are, without judging or labeling them. This can lead to a more open and tolerant attitude towards the people we meet in our daily lives.

4. Develop self-compassion: By practicing metta meditation, we also learn to be kinder to ourselves and to treat ourselves with love and respect, recognizing that we too need understanding and support.
5. Promote emotional well-being: Regular practice of metta meditation has been associated with greater life satisfaction, a lower tendency to anxiety and depression, and an overall improvement in emotional well-being.

In conclusion, practicing metta meditation regularly can have a significant impact on the way we interact with others and the quality of our relationships.

By cultivating empathy and compassion, we can enhance our social lives and help create a more loving and supportive environment around us.

In-Depth Practice Exercise: Metta Meditation for Relationships

1. Find a quiet place and a comfortable position to meditate.
2. Close your eyes and bring your attention to your breath. Concentrate on inhaling and exhaling, letting your mind settle.
3. Now, imagine yourself radiating love and kindness. Mentally repeat these phrases: "May I be happy, may I be healthy, may I be safe, may I live with ease."
4. Once you feel love and kindness for yourself, extend this loving energy to a friend or family member. Visualize this person in your mind and repeat the same sentences, replacing "I" with their name or "you".
5. Keep extending this love and kindness to people further and further apart: colleagues, acquaintances, strangers, and even people with whom you have difficulty in relationships. Repeat the phrases for each of these people,

wishing them happiness, health, safety and ease.

6. Finally, extend this love and kindness to all people in the world, without exception. Imagine love and kindness spreading in all directions, touching every living thing.

7. When you feel ready, bring your attention back to your breath. Take a moment to reflect on the love and kindness you have cultivated during this meditation and how you can bring it into your daily relationships.

8. Slowly bring your awareness back to the room and to your body, gently moving your fingers and toes. When you feel ready, open your eyes and finish the meditation.

Regularly practicing metta meditation can help you develop empathy and compassion for others, improving your interpersonal relationships and your ability to communicate with clarity and kindness. Remember that meditation is a skill that develops over time, so be patient with yourself and keep practicing.

Practicing metta meditation regularly can bring numerous benefits to our emotional and relationship well-being. Metta meditation, also known as "loving-kindness meditation," has as its main goal the development of empathy and compassion, both towards ourselves and towards others.

CHAPTER 21: MEDITATION AND HEALTH: PREVENTING AND CURING DISEASE

Meditation is a millenary practice that has been shown to have beneficial effects not only on our mind and emotions, but also on our physical health.

Numerous scientific studies have highlighted how meditation can help prevent and treat various diseases and disorders, contributing to our general well-being.

1. Meditation and the immune system

Regular meditation practice can strengthen the immune system, making us more resistant to infection and disease. Meditation reduces stress and inflammation in the body, two factors that can weaken the immune system and increase susceptibility to disease.

2. Meditation and cardiovascular health

Meditation has been associated with better cardiovascular health, reducing the risk of heart disease, stroke and high blood pressure. Meditation practice can lower blood pressure, improve endothelial function and reduce oxidative stress, all of which contribute to heart health.

3. Meditation and chronic pain

Meditation can be an effective tool for managing chronic pain. Practicing mindfulness and acceptance can help reduce your perception of pain and increase your tolerance for physical discomfort.

4. Meditation and sleep disorders

Meditation can help improve the quality of sleep and fight insomnia, reducing the anxiety and tension that often prevent you from sleeping well. Meditation practice before bed can help relax the mind and body, making it easier to fall asleep and maintain sleep.

Practical exercise: Meditation for deep relaxation and healing

1. Find a quiet, comfortable place to sit or lie down. Make sure you are not disturbed for at least 15-20 minutes.
2. Close your eyes and bring your attention to your breath. Observe the natural flow of air as it enters and exits your nostrils.
3. With each inhalation, imagine yourself bringing healing energy into your body. With each exhalation, let go of tension, worry, and pain.
4. Now, bring your attention to each part of your body, one at a time, starting with your head and working your way down to your feet. Take a few breaths for each part, imagining that you are relaxing it and releasing it from any tension or pain.
5. Visualize a warm, bright light surrounding your entire body. Imagine that this light has healing and regenerative properties, capable of restoring health and well-being to every cell of your body.
6. Hold this visualization for a few minutes,

feeling the healing light penetrate deep into your body, regenerating and strengthening your immune system, reducing inflammation and promoting healing.

7. Now, imagine this healing light expanding beyond your body, reaching your mind and spirit as well. Let the light bring peace, calm and serenity to your thoughts and emotions.

8. Take a few minutes to assimilate the beneficial effects of this meditation, feeling the connection between mind, body and spirit and the power of inner healing.

9. When you feel ready, bring your attention back to your breath, take a few deep breaths, and slowly open your eyes again.

Remember that regular meditation practice is crucial to reaping its long-term health benefits. Set aside time each day to take care of yourself and cultivate physical, mental, and emotional well-being through meditation.

CHAPTER 22: MEDITATION AND AGING: SLOWING TIME AND IMPROVING QUALITY OF LIFE

Aging is a natural process involving physical, mental and emotional changes throughout life.

Meditation can help slow some of these changes and improve quality of life in older people by helping to reduce stress, improve memory and attention, increase energy and vitality, and promote greater self-awareness.

The Benefits of Meditation on Aging . Meditation offers several benefits for aging, including:

- Stress reduction: Chronic stress can accelerate cellular aging and increase the risk of age-related diseases. Meditation helps reduce stress by improving your ability to handle stressful situations and promoting relaxation.
- Improved memory and attention: Meditation can help improve memory and attention, which tend to decline

with aging. Regular meditation practice can increase brain plasticity and help maintain an agile mind.

- Increased energy and vitality: Meditation can improve the quality of sleep, reduce fatigue and increase energy, helping older people feel more energetic and vital.
- Promoting self-awareness: Meditation can help develop greater self-awareness and a better understanding of one's emotions, thoughts and needs, promoting acceptance of the aging process and emotional well-being.

Gratitude meditation is a great practice for older people, as it helps focus on the positive aspects of life and recognize the gifts and blessings one has, despite the challenges of aging.

To get the maximum benefits from meditation, it is important to integrate it into daily life. Here are some suggestions for integrating meditation into the daily life of older people.

- Choose a quiet time and place for meditation, preferably away from distractions and noise. It can be useful to create a space dedicated to meditation, with a cushion or a comfortable chair.

- Start with short meditation sessions, even as little as 5-10 minutes a day, and gradually increase the length of the sessions over time.

- Try different meditation techniques to find the one that works best for you. Some older people may prefer guided meditation, while others may find mindfulness meditation or breathing meditation more helpful.

- Involve friends or family members in your meditation practice, by creating a meditation group or by attending meditation classes and retreats.

- Remember that meditation is a practice and it takes time and effort to see results. Be patient and kind to yourself during the process.

In conclusion, meditation offers numerous benefits for older people, helping to slow down the aging process and improve the quality of life. By regularly integrating meditation into your daily life, you will be able to experience increased self-awareness, reduced stress, and improved physical and mental health.

Practical exercise: Meditation on gratitude
Here's how to practice gratitude meditation:

1. Find a quiet, comfortable place to sit or lie down.

2. Close your eyes and take a few deep breaths, focusing on the sensation of the air moving in and out of your nostrils.

3. Bring to mind three things you are grateful for in your life. These can be relationships, experiences, material items, or whatever makes you feel grateful and happy.

4. Now, imagine holding these three things in your heart, feeling gratitude spreading throughout your body and mind.

5. Continue to focus on gratitude for a few minutes, allowing this feeling to fill you with joy and appreciation for life.

6. When you feel ready, bring your attention back to the breath and slowly return to your normal awareness. Take a moment to reflect on the feeling of gratitude you experienced while meditating.

CHAPTER 23: MEDITATION FOR CHILDREN: DEVELOPING MINDFULNESS AND SOCIAL-EMOTIONAL SKILLS

Introduction to meditation for children
Meditation isn't just for adults; even children can benefit enormously from this practice. Teaching children to meditate can help them develop greater self-awareness, manage stress and emotions, and improve their social and emotional skills.

Additionally, meditation can help children focus better and improve their academic performance.

Benefits of meditation for children
The benefits of meditation for children include:

- Improved concentration and attention
- Reduction of stress and anxiety
- Developing awareness of one's own emotions and the ability to manage them
- Improved social skills, such as empathy and communication
- Enhancement of creativity and imagination
- Improved sleep quality
- Reduction of symptoms of disorders such as hyperactivity and attention deficit disorder

Meditation techniques suitable for children

There are several meditation techniques suitable for children, including:

- Breathing Meditation: Teaching children to focus on their breath can help them calm down and relax. Ask your child to inhale deeply and exhale slowly, focusing on the flow of air going in and out of the nostrils.
- Guided Meditation: Guided meditations are stories or descriptions that help children imagine a relaxing place or situation. This type of meditation can be especially effective for children who have vivid imaginations.
- Body Awareness Meditation: This technique helps children become aware of different parts of their body and the sensations they experience. Ask the child to focus on each part of the body, starting with the feet and working their way up to the head, noticing the sensations that arise.

Practical guided meditation exercise you can do with a child:

1. Have the child sit or lie down comfortably in a quiet, distraction-free place.

2. Have your child close their eyes and focus on their breathing, slowly inhaling and exhaling.
3. Tell your child a story or describe a relaxing place, such as a beach, forest, or enchanted garden. Use evocative and detailed words to help the child imagine the place you are describing.
4. Ask the child to imagine walking in the place you have described, feeling the sounds, scents and sensations that surround him.
5. After spending a few minutes exploring this imaginary place, invite the child to focus again on his breathing, slowly inhaling and exhaling.
6. Ask the child to take with him the feeling of calm and peace he experienced in the imaginary place and to keep it in his heart as he returns to reality.
7. Invite the child to slowly open his eyes and become aware of his body and the surrounding environment.
8. Ask the child to share the meditation experience by discussing what they have seen, heard, and learned.

Encouraging children to practice meditation regularly can help them develop positive habits and better manage stress and emotions in their daily lives. Through meditation, children can learn to cultivate mindfulness, empathy, and communication, making them more balanced and happy adults.

CHAPTER 24: MEDITATION FOR THE PREGNANT WOMAN: POSTURE AND BREATHING

Pregnancy is a time of profound change and profound transformation for women. Meditation can offer numerous benefits for pregnant women, helping to find balance, well-being and serenity in this important period of life.

1. Posture: Posture is crucial for an effective and comfortable meditation practice during pregnancy. It's important to choose a comfortable position that supports your back and belly. You can opt for a straight back chair or a meditation cushion. Maintain an upright but relaxed position with shoulders back and neck stretched out.

2. Breathing: Breathing is a powerful tool for calming the mind and relaxing the body. During pregnancy, it's especially important to pay attention to your breathing, as it can help reduce stress and improve oxygen flow to the fetus. Practicing deep breathing exercises, such as

diaphragmatic breathing, can be very helpful.

Pregnancy is a time of great physical and emotional changes for a woman. During these nine months, it's crucial that you find a way to stay calm and deal with any stress and anxiety that may arise. Meditation is an invaluable tool in achieving this goal, as it can help improve the mother-to-be's physical and emotional well-being.

Here are some benefits of meditation during pregnancy:

1. Stress Reduction: Meditation helps reduce stress levels through focus on the breath and present moment awareness. This allows the woman to detach herself from negative thoughts and worries about the pregnancy, promoting an atmosphere of calm and serenity.

2. Improved sleep: During pregnancy, sleep quality can be impaired due to hormonal changes and physical discomfort. Meditation can help improve sleep by relaxing the body and mind, promoting deeper and more rejuvenating rest.

3. Strengthening the mother-baby bond: Meditation can help strengthen the bond between mother and baby through awareness of the physical sensations and emotions that accompany pregnancy. This heightened awareness helps create a sense of deep connection between the mother and her unborn child.

4. Managing Emotions: Meditation allows you to observe and accept the emotions that may arise during pregnancy, without judgment or resistance. This mindful approach helps to manage emotions more effectively and to find inner calm and balance.

5. Preparing for childbirth: Meditation can be a valuable tool in preparing for childbirth, as it helps develop greater awareness of the body and breath. These skills can be used

during labor and delivery to manage pain and stay focused in the present moment.

Incorporating meditation into your daily routine during pregnancy can bring a number of benefits, including increased calmness and serenity. Even just a few minutes a day can make a difference, helping the expectant mother to find inner balance and to experience pregnancy in a more harmonious way.

Practical exercise:

1. Find a quiet, comfortable place to sit or lie down, making sure you have adequate back and belly support.
2. Close your eyes and bring your attention to your breath. Notice how air moves in and out of your nostrils and how your abdomen rises and falls with each breath.
3. Start practicing diaphragmatic breathing, inhaling slowly and exhaling in a controlled manner. Imagine that your diaphragm is a balloon that inflates with each inhalation and deflates with each exhalation.
4. Continue to breathe deeply and calmly, trying to relax every part of your body, from head to toe.
5. Now, imagine a warm, soothing light surrounding your body and your baby. This light brings love, protection and nourishment to both of you.
6. Remain in this meditation for at least 5-10 minutes, or longer if you wish.
7. When you're ready, slowly bring your attention to the present, gently moving your fingers and toes. Open your eyes and take a moment to feel the connection with your baby and the sense of inner well-being.

CHAPTER 25: MEDITATION AND SPIRITUALITY: THE PATH TO ENLIGHTENMENT

Meditation is closely linked to spirituality, as it represents a tool for deepening self-understanding and the reality that surrounds us. Through meditative practice, we can go beyond the mind and its limitations, allowing us to experience a deeper connection with our spiritual nature and true self.

The path to enlightenment is an individual and personal path, which develops through constant dedication to meditation practice and exploration of one's inner self. However, there are some common aspects that can be useful for those venturing down this path:

1. Present Moment Awareness: Through meditation, we learn to live in the here and now, appreciating the present moment and detaching ourselves from worries and fears related to the past or future.

2. Observation Without Judgment: Meditation teaches us to observe our thoughts and emotions without judgment or resistance, allowing us to accept our inner experience as it is and to develop a greater understanding of ourselves.
3. Cultivating Compassion: Meditative practice helps us develop compassion and empathy for others, recognizing that all living beings share the same desire for happiness and the same aversion to pain.
4. Connect with Inner Wisdom: Meditation allows us to access our inner wisdom and develop a deeper view of reality, going beyond superficial appearances and illusions created by the mind.

Practical exercise: Meditation on the nature of the self.
This meditative exercise is intended to bring attention to the nature of the self and to foster an understanding of our true essence, beyond the temporary identities and roles we assume in daily life.

1. Find a quiet, comfortable place to sit, with your back straight but relaxed. Close your eyes and start focusing on your breathing, not trying to change or control it. Let your mind settle down and relax.
2. Now, start thinking about the question: "Who am I?" Without looking for an immediate answer, observe how this question resonates within you and what thoughts or emotions arise.
3. When you find yourself being carried away by thoughts, return to the question: "Who am I?" and continue to observe the answers that emerge, without judgment or attachment.
4. As your meditation progresses, you may begin to notice how your identity is actually a whole of roles, beliefs

and habits you have adopted over time. These temporary identities can change and transform, but beyond them, there is a deeper and more unalterable nature, your true essence.

5. Try to come closer to this awareness of your true self, letting go of the temporary labels and identities that limit you. Immerse yourself in the feeling of freedom and space that opens up when you recognize your essential nature.

6. Conclude the meditation by bringing your attention back to the breath, and slowly return to your awareness of your body and surroundings. Take a moment to reflect on the experience and integrate the teachings into your daily life.

Remember that the path to enlightenment is a personal and unique path for each one. Continue to practice meditation regularly and experiment with different techniques, always maintaining an attitude of openness, curiosity and compassion.

Over time, you will discover how meditation can help you cultivate a deep connection with your true nature and transform your life into an authentic expression of your spirituality.

CHAPTER 26: INTEGRATING MEDITATION INTO DAILY LIFE

Meditation is not only a practice that takes place at a certain time or place, it is also a mindset that can be integrated into every aspect of your life. In this chapter, we'll explore some strategies for bringing the benefits of meditation into your everyday life.

1. Create a daily routine: Establishing a daily meditation routine can help you make the practice a natural part of your life. Find a time and place that works for you, and try to meditate at the same times each day.

2. Be present in daily activities: Meditation teaches us to be fully present in the present moment. Try to bring this awareness into your daily activities, such as eating, walking, or showering. Pay attention to your senses and physical sensations, and try to stay connected to the present moment.

3. Practice Kindness and Compassion: Meditation can help you cultivate an attitude of kindness and compassion

toward yourself and others. Try to bring these qualities into your daily life, offering kindness and support to the people you meet and practicing self-compassion when you're feeling judgmental or critical of yourself.

4. Take breaks for meditation: Take short breaks throughout the day to meditate, even if it's just for a few minutes. This can help you reconnect with the present moment, relax and recharge your batteries.

5. Be aware of your thoughts and emotions: Try to observe your thoughts and emotions throughout the day without judging or identifying with them. This practice can help you develop greater self-awareness and better deal with daily stress and challenges.

By integrating meditation into your daily life, you will be able to reap the maximum benefits from the practice and come ever closer to a balanced, joyful and meaningful life. Remember that meditation is a personal journey and that everyone has their own pace and ways of learning.

Keep exploring and experimenting, and you'll see how meditation can transform your life in surprising and wonderful ways.

To further explore integrating meditation into your daily life, we'll look at some techniques and tips that can help you incorporate mindfulness and awareness into every aspect of your life.

1. Informal Meditation: In addition to formal meditation, which is practiced in a calm, structured environment, informal meditation can be practiced during daily activities. For example, you can focus on your breathing as you wait for the bus, observe your thoughts as you stand in line at the grocery store, or pay attention to physical sensations as you wash the dishes.

2. Use a mindfulness reminder: To remind yourself to stay

mindful and present throughout the day, you could use reminders. For example, you might set a reminder on your phone to remind you to pause and meditate or choose an everyday item, like a ring or bracelet, that reminds you to bring awareness into the present moment.

3. Cultivating Gratitude: Gratitude is a powerful emotion that can help you develop a more positive attitude and appreciate the little joys of everyday life. You can cultivate gratitude by meditating on what you are grateful for each day or by keeping a gratitude journal in which you write down the things you value in your life.

4. Practice active listening: Meditation can help you develop greater awareness of yourself and others. One of the ways to put this awareness into practice is active listening, which consists in paying full attention to what the other is saying, without judgment and without interrupting. This can improve your relationships and help you develop empathy and understanding for others.

5. Exercise patience: Meditation teaches us to be patient with ourselves and with others. Try to bring this quality into your daily life, learning to accept difficult situations and to treat the people you meet with kindness and patience.

By integrating these techniques and tips into your daily life, you can further deepen your meditation practice and bring the benefits of meditation into every aspect of your life. Remember that constant practice and an open mind are key to achieving lasting results and transforming your life experience.

CHAPTER 27: CONSOLIDATING MEDITATION PRACTICE: HELPFUL TIPS AND RESOURCES

To consolidate your meditation practice and continue to progress on your path of inner growth, it is important to adopt some strategies and take advantage of the resources available. Below, you will find some helpful tips and resources that will help you maintain and improve your meditation practice over time.

1. Establish a daily routine: Regularity is key to establishing a solid meditation practice. Try to set aside a specific time of day for meditation, preferably in the morning or evening when your mind is at its calmest. Maintaining a daily routine will help you form a habit of meditating and make it easier to integrate meditation into your life.

2. Join Meditation Groups or Retreats: Joining a local meditation group or participating in a meditation retreat can be a very helpful experience to deepen your practice and share your experiences with other practitioners.

Meditation groups and retreats offer an environment of support and encouragement, as well as providing an opportunity to learn from expert teachers and connect with like-minded people.

3. Experiment with Different Techniques: Because every person is unique, it's possible that some meditation techniques will work better for you than others. Don't be afraid to experiment with different forms of meditation to find out which ones suit your needs and preferences best. Variety can also help keep the practice fresh and interesting.

4. Learn from books, courses, and teachers: Continue to learn more about meditation by reading books, attending courses, or listening to teachings from spiritual teachers. This will help you develop a deeper understanding of various meditation techniques and philosophies and provide you with additional tools to enhance your practice.

5. Keep a Meditation Journal: Recording your experiences and observations after each meditation session can be an effective way to monitor your progress and reflect on your personal discoveries. A meditation journal can also help you identify any obstacles or challenges you may be experiencing and find solutions to overcome them.

6. Be patient and kind to yourself: Meditation is a growing and learning process that takes time, patience, and dedication. Don't be discouraged if you don't see immediate results or if you encounter difficulties along the way. Remember to be kind and compassionate to yourself and accept your unique path of spiritual growth and development.

Using these tips and resources, you can solidify your your meditation practice and continue to progress on your path of personal and spiritual growth. In addition to these tips, it's important to stay open to new experiences and knowledge, as meditation is a constantly evolving journey.

7. Listen to Guided Meditation Podcasts and Recordings: Guided Meditation podcasts and recordings are a great resource for expanding your knowledge about meditation and learning new techniques. You can listen to them on the go, during a break from work, or before bed to relax.

8. Use meditation apps: There are several meditation apps available that offer a variety of features, including guided meditations, customizable timers, meditation challenges, and progress tracking. These apps can be a useful tool in making your practice more accessible and motivating.

9. Seek support from friends and family: Sharing your meditation practice with friends and family can be an effective way to gain support, encouragement, and understanding. Also, you may find that some of them are interested in joining you in meditation practice, thus creating a shared experience.

10. Attend Workshops and Conferences: Events such as meditation workshops and conferences provide an invaluable opportunity to learn from experts, ask questions, and connect with other practitioners. Attending these events will help you expand your knowledge and network in the field of meditation.

11. Don't forget the value of silence: While it's important to use external resources to deepen your practice, don't underestimate the power of silence and solitude. Take time to meditate in silence, without external distractions or stimuli, to cultivate a deeper connection with yourself and your meditation practice.

By following these tips and taking advantage of the resources available, you will be able to strengthen and enrich your meditation practice, experiencing the many benefits that meditation can offer on a physical, mental and emotional level. Remember that meditation is a personal and unique journey, and that progress comes through consistent practice and commitment.

THANKSGIVING

I wish to express my sincere gratitude to all of you who have accompanied this journey into the world of meditation. Thank you for believing in the value of this book and choosing it as a guide for your personal and spiritual growth.

Special thanks go to all the friends and family who have supported and encouraged me throughout the writing of this work. Your trust in me and your unconditional support have been instrumental in reaching this milestone.

Thanks also to those who, through their experience and wisdom, have taught me the art of meditation. Your lessons and teachings have been invaluable in deepening my understanding of this age-old practice and in passing it on to others through this book.

Finally, special thanks to all of you readers who have purchased and read this book. Your curiosity and your desire to grow have been my inspiration to write this work. I hope that the pages you have read have offered you new perspectives and useful tools to enrich your life and your spiritual journey.

I wish you to find peace, harmony and happiness through the practice of meditation. May the benefits of this practice illuminate every aspect of your existence and guide you towards a more mindful, balanced and fulfilling life.
Thank you with all my heart,
Jean-Michel Ps

THANK YOU

Printed in Great Britain
by Amazon